Surviving the Storm

One Woman's Journey through Vulvar Cancer

LAURA L. TORRES

WESTBOW
PRESS®
A DIVISION OF THOMAS NELSON
& ZONDERVAN

WestBow Press books may be ordered through booksellers or by contacting:

WestBow Press
A Division of Thomas Nelson & Zondervan
1663 Liberty Drive
Bloomington, IN 47403
www.westbowpress.com
1 (866) 928-1240

ISBN: 978-1-9736-1525-5 (sc)
ISBN: 978-1-9736-1524-8 (hc)
ISBN: 978-1-9736-1526-2 (e)

Library of Congress Control Number: 2018900715

Print information available on the last page.

WestBow Press rev. date: 3/21/2018

I am so thankful for the comfort and peace God gave me throughout this fight against the storm raging inside of me. I am so thankful for my family and friends, who are an extension of His love. They were the gentle reminders that God was there—always. "I am even thankful for my cancer" because without it I would not have come to the place I am today.

God bless you all.

"To my family and friends, I love you with all of my heart"

Contents

Chapter 1

Cancer. What can I say other than it stinks? You never imagine it will happen to you. When it does, the emotional roller coaster is merciless. Imagine it: one minute you are a healthy individual who is sitting and waiting for the doctor to come in and tell you there is nothing to worry about, and two seconds later, you are being diagnosed with cancer. It leaves you with a sinking feeling in the pit of your gut. After a few moments pass, your body will likely go into shock, shaking uncontrollably, as your mind continues to digest that six-letter word. I had never really understood my patients when they described feeling so disconnected, like they were just going through the motions. But I understand it now.

Initial Social Media Post

Well, I definitely did not get the answers I wanted. But God is good, and I have faith that His will will be done. Just a little mind-numbing at the moment. So far, the diagnosis is metastatic squamous cell carcinoma with an unknown primary site. Hoping the PET scan on Friday will pinpoint that. I would just ask for continued prayers for me and my family. I love you all. I am so blessed to have such a great family and friends.

I was all alone when I got the news. Metastatic vulvar cancer. I had worked in the medical field for over ten years, so of course I knew just enough to be dangerous, mostly to myself. I knew *metastatic* was not a good word. It increased the odds that this would have a bad outcome. I already knew I was going to be waiting to see where it had spread to. It scared me more to have to tell my kids I had cancer than it scared me to know I had cancer.

The Lord is my strength and my shield; my
heart trust in Him, and I am helped.
—Psalm 28:7

I was mentally kicking myself in the rear for not finding out what was going on with myself sooner. The lump had been there for months, but it didn't hurt, so I didn't worry about it. What was I thinking? I was really more worried about how my kids were going to take this news than anything. I was already set to hit this head-on, but my children were going to be devastated. After my gynecologist went over all of my test results and she reexamined me, I was supposed to be getting dressed, but instead I just sat there, alone and numb. My brain was going a mile a minute. My thoughts were being pulled like taffy in twelve different directions. I had cancer, but all I kept thinking was that I didn't have time to have cancer. I had just completed my bachelor's degree in health administration and management. I was a busy single mother who still had four kids at home. I worked over forty hours a week; I seriously did not have time for cancer.

Thankfully, I was saved from my thoughts by a knock at the door. Dr. Green was standing there. Not only was she the doctor I worked with, but also she had become my friend. She had come to the office to support me because she knew I was there alone. She entered the exam room and gave me a big hug. I have to tell you that hugs are great. I really needed that one. I just didn't know how much I'd needed it until she was there.

We talked for a while, and then I figured it was time to go home.

I know I drove home from the office visit, but I certainly don't remember the drive. Before I left the parking lot, I called my boyfriend, Lyle, and gave him the news. He was my cheerleader through all of this. Our circumstances didn't allow him to be with me often, but he was always just a phone call away. He assured me we were going to get through this, and he told me often how much he loved me.

After that phone call, I knew I had to get all of my kids together, so I sent each of them a text, asking them to be at the house because I needed to talk to them. I remember thinking about what I was going to say and how I was going to say it, "but one thing it promised to do, no matter how I arranged the words, was to crush their spirit, which was the last thing I wanted to do." Everyone can relate to this in one way or another. It doesn't have to be cancer; even talking with kids about the death of a loved one

Humble yourselves before the Lord, and he will lift you up.
—James 4:10

can be overwhelming. I wanted to give them a message of hope, of blessings, and of God's love, even though I knew in my heart they would want to blame God. They would be angry.

I honestly didn't think I could bear it. I knew in my mind that I had to find a way to keep things together and show them how strong I was. I needed to deliver a spirited fight song, a war cry against cancer. I needed them to feel as if we were going to be the toughest team to beat.

Nothing came out the way I'd rehearsed it. I just blurted it out: "I have cancer." They sat there for a moment, stunned, but once it sank in, we talked..." they cried, and we hugged *a lot*. I believe we have been each other's support system through this journey. I was, and still am, open and honest with them about everything. I promised them that there would be no surprises. They would be getting the news regarding my health the same time I would be. I didn't want them wondering if there was something I wasn't telling them. My children were all old enough to know what was going on. I even explained some things to my granddaughter, Lily, who was only two and a half at the time of my diagnosis. She understood enough. She knew her *geema* (her special name for me) had *owies* and was sick. She always gave me lots of hugs. She would come up to me, hold my head in her little hands, and tell me she loved me so much. It would melt my heart. Still does. God was blessing me throughout this fight through that beautiful little girl.

The first night after I was given my diagnosis was, in my mind, probably the longest night I have ever endured. I lay there taking a mental tally of the things I had accomplished in my life. There had already been so many circumstances in my life that were testing my faith, but cancer was the biggest by far. I wept as I talked with God. I just kept thinking, *How can He keep allowing things like this to happen in my life? What am I doing wrong?* There had to be something I wasn't seeing, something I wasn't doing. I read and reread the book of Job. Job lost everything, yet he was

*Do not be anxious about anything, but in everything by prayer
and petition, with Thanksgiving, present your requests to God.
And the peace of God, which transcends all understanding,
will guard your hearts and your minds in Christ Jesus.
—Philippians 4:6–7*

firm in his faith. "He remained faithful and didn't question God's plan for his life at the time he was experiencing tremendous loss and hardship. His own wife was telling him to "curse God and give up!", to which he responded "Shall we accept good from God, and not trouble? Job 2:10b" In despair, Job did curse the day he was born, but even Jesus asked God the Father "My God, My God, Why have You forsaken me? Why are you so far from saving me, so far from my cries of anguish? Psalm 22:1" Now here I was, crying like a baby and asking, "Why? Why? Why?"

Now, I am in no way comparing myself to Job and the trials and losses he endured, although I certainly felt like him for a brief moment. But I didn't want to get stuck having a pity party for myself, because I was afraid I would not be able to pull myself out of it. My thoughts flashed back to the things I would tell my patients when they were struggling, which was about how they looked at things, their perspective and spiritual mind-set, I'd told them, was half the battle.

After I entertained the idea of feeling sorry for myself, I made my mind up, I was going into this battle with a joyful heart. I was ready to fight this with grace and dignity, and let me tell you that when you are dealing with vulvar cancer, dignity kind of goes out the window fairly quickly. I was able to hold on to the grace, though. I am not saying there were not ups and downs along the way, but I am saying that God is good all the time. When I was afraid, I prayed and was blanketed with peace and comfort like I had never experienced before. I was never alone through this. He was always with me.

It is so important to have a good support system when you have a cancer diagnosis—honestly, with *any* diagnosis that becomes life-changing. That could be heart disease, diabetes, a neurological disorder, or anything really. If it changes your life, then it is big. If you don't have a family, a friend, a church home, or someone to talk to, seek out support. I reached out to my uncle John, who is a pastor at a local church, and I prayed with him and my aunt Marla. It was powerful. The support you receive will make a huge difference in your life and will form bonds with people you

Every good and perfect gift is from above, coming down from the Father of the heavenly lights, who does not change like shifting shadows.
—James 1:17

will know forever. But you can also be the supporter who is serving others with love and compassion. I know that before this diagnosis, I wasn't doing that nearly as well as I should have been.

With a cancer diagnosis comes an influx of information from every direction. It was definitely a system overload for my brain, and I have to be honest, I didn't pay attention to most of it. I certainly didn't research anything on the Internet, because I swear that anytime you look up an illness or a symptom, it tells you that you are dying.

I didn't want to hear that from my doctors, so I certainly didn't want to read it on the computer. I avoided getting caught up in percentages and ratios and reading statistics. I concentrated on me, my fight, and what the doctors were doing to keep me alive.

I also had to avoid what I am sure almost all patients newly diagnosed with cancer go through, and that is the well-meaning friends and family who claim to have the magical cure for cancer. Now, I will never say that diet doesn't help. We can always expect our bodies to care for us the way we care for them. If you are putting garbage into your body, you are going to get garbage as a result. You have to find a way to respectfully thank your well-meaning friends and family and pray about all things on a daily basis. They are just afraid for you. They will share cures that involve vitamin C overload and the story about the "one guy" who just juiced carrots and turned orange and his cancer was amazingly gone. There is always that "one guy" cure. Again, I am not knocking it, because there is always going to be that one person whom it does work for. Being from the medical world, I do believe God gave doctors the knowledge and abilities to do the great things they are capable of. I also believe that God put everything here on earth for a purpose, so I am a firm believer in the medicinal properties of herbs and foods. I have confidence in the fact that there is a good blend between modern medicines and natural therapies. The positive outcome can be greater, in my opinion, when you combine the two. Fortunately for me, I had an excellent team of doctors at Froedtert and they were open to

When you pass through the waters, I will be with you; and when you pass through the rivers, they will not sweep over you. When you walk through the fire, you will not be burned; the flames will not set you ablaze.
—Isaiah 43:2

5

discuss natural alternatives to supplement conventional medical methods and treatments. I know, the medical world still seems to be learning about how all the "natural" treatments fit into the equations. At least they are not blind to them. My health-care providers were open to the possibilities of "other" methods working in conjunction with their treatments.

Needless to say, I didn't choose the all-natural treatment option, as I have seen it go terribly wrong for many people. But I am certainly not saying that if this is your choice it is wrong or won't work. It just wasn't the right choice for me. I prayed on this very hard, and God's answer was very clear to me. We talked with the doctors, the nurses, and the pharmacist. We weighed our options carefully. The medications they were recommending that I take during treatments did not amount to a complete arsenal, but they were enough for me, since I don't like taking pills. I was that woman who always said that if I ever developed a heart condition and had to take medication every day to treat it, I would probably die, because I wouldn't want to take the medicine. Well, guess what? I am that woman who developed a heart condition and has to take medication for it every day. How ironic is that? Who says God doesn't have a sense of humor? Not I.

Chapter 2

I had my cancer diagnosis. The last piece of the puzzle was to have a PET (positron emission tomography) scan done, to see if I lit up like a Christmas tree or not. The prayer was not to light up. The doctors already knew that my lymph nodes in the right groin area were obliterated, but now the twenty-thousand-dollar question was, how far had the cancer spread? If it had spread too far, my care would be palliative, and all of this talk of surgery and treatment options would be for nothing. At age forty-six, I was certainly not ready for that. Palliative care is the medical term for when care is provided for comfort, without actually treating the disease. In other words, palliative care is used to make you comfortable for the rest of your short natural life. My mind did focus for a moment on the possibility that this could be the end of the road for me. It was unimaginable for me to think that at my age, with my kids not all being adults yet, my grandchildren still being so small, and my spirit still being so full of life, my care may be palliative.

Three months prior, I'd thought I had life all figured out. Funny how I kept being reminded that I am not the one in control. I try to always look at the humorous side of things. One of my previous prayers was for God to take away my student loan debt. I had to laugh. I just raised my eyes to the sky and told God that this was not the way I wanted my debt to disappear. I wasn't ready for the express train to heaven. I thought, *Fine, I will not complain about student loans again.*

I spent a few nights asking a lot of what-if questions. Those questions didn't really help solve anything. One minute we are here; the next minute we are gone. That is the only answer that I kept coming up with. Only God knows the hour of our deaths. Why was I worrying about it? I prayed,

> *But the fruit of the Spirit is love, joy, peace, patience, kindness, goodness, faithfulness, gentleness and self-control. Against such things there is no law.*
> *—Galatians 5:22–23*

a lot. I renewed my walk with the Lord. I knew that before all of this, my relationship with God was not as strong or as personal as it should have been. I knew being a good person was not enough. I knew it. Cancer was a wake-up call for me. And for that, I am thankful. Yes, I am thankful for my cancer.

I know that there are people in my life who have pulled away from me because of my faith, and I have had to learn that that it is their choice. I cannot change because they chose to do so. But I can tell you, God did not leave my side, not for one moment. I would not be where I am today without Him.

Social Media Post

PET scan today. Nervous for results ... but one bit of good news is that they do think the cancer is localized, which is good. The scan today will be the deciding factor. Thank you so much for all of your prayers. I love all of you and am so blessed. Please continue to pray not only for me but also for my family. Thank you so much. God is good. Prayer is powerful.

I completed my PET scan and anxiously awaited the news. Every doctor who had examined me thus far was waiting anxiously. My cancer was rare, so I think that in part, it was a learning experience. The other part was the fact that I was friends with many of my doctors, so it was also personal for them.

I remember standing in a local secondhand store, trying to get my mind off of everything, when my phone rang. My heart froze. I couldn't answer the phone fast enough, my fingers fumbling to swipe the right way on the screen. I was terrified of the news I was about to receive. My hands were shaking as I said hello. The next thing everyone in the store heard was me crying out, "Thank you, Jesus!" Tears rolled down my face. I ran to my

No temptation has seized you except what is common to man. And God is faithful; He will not let you be tempted beyond what you can bear. But when you are tempted, He will also provide a way out so that you can stand up under it.
—1 Corinthians 10:13

boyfriend, Lyle, and hugged him, saying, probably louder than I realized at the time, "The cancer has *not* spread! It is all localized. The cancer has *not* spread! Thank you, Jesus. Our prayers were answered." The cancer had, in fact, stayed in a nice, tight-knit community in my right groin and vulva. The doctors did not see cancer anywhere else in my body.

Praise the Lord! Pure, unadulterated joy. That is what I felt. For now, no palliative care. Now we were going to plan our attack. I could hear the horns blowing in the back of my mind: "Duh, duh, duh, da, da, da … charge!"

Finally, I let go of Lyle for fear I was cutting off his air supply by squeezing him so tight. Neither one of us was able to wipe the smiles from our faces that day.

Social Media Post

So, good news … I can't win a one-in-a-million lottery, but I can get a rare cancer. The great news is that it's all localized. That is great for my prognosis. No cancer anywhere else. Praise God. Please keep praying. I see the oncologist on Thursday. I am pretty sure I will be having surgery before treatments. But it is definitely the scan result we were praying for! Thank you. I love you all. I was already set up to meet a great local oncologist. Now that I have some peace of mind, as far as the cancer being localized, my life can return to being as normal as it possibly can be.

I will say of the Lord, "He is my refuge and my
fortress, my God, in whom I trust."
—Psalm 91:2

Chapter 3

Social Media Post

First oncology appointment today. Oh boy. Will give an update later. All I can say is, God is good, and everyone's prayers have been heard. Still a long scary road ahead. Keep praying, please. I want to extend a special thank-you to my brother, Andrew Bodnar. I love you. Thank you for the visit, the plans to fix things, and the air filters. I truly enjoyed spending time with you. And my mom, Sandra Hurtt, and my grandmother Betty, for coming Saturday to visit and help with groceries … thank you so much. I couldn't ask for better family and friends. And my love, Lyle Torres, thank you for holding me, loving me, and praying for me. My outlook is good, my faith is strong, my family and friends are woven tightly together to support me, and God is good, all the time. I am a little emotional lately with all of the well-wishes, prayers, and love. This is a very humbling and eye-opening journey.

The local oncologist we saw was great. He gave us information on his surgical plan, my hospitalization time, and aftercare and follow-up. I had made the appointment to see him right after my diagnosis because I wanted to get a jump on things.

It was suggested to me that I get a second opinion because of the rareness of my cancer and to ensure I was comfortable with my surgical options and treatment plan. I set up a second appointment in Milwaukee at Froedtert & the Medical College's Cancer Care Center. A second opinion sounded like a good idea to me, not that there was anything wrong with the plan the first surgical oncologist had laid out for me. After I had seen

*Therefore, encourage one another and build each
other up, just as in fact, you are doing.*
—1 Thessalonians 5:11

both doctors, it was very clear to both me and Lyle where we would be seeking out my care. One extremely important part of your treatment has to be how comfortable you are in the environment the health-care providers create for you. You have to feel as if those taking care of you have your best interests at heart, that you are not just a number or a surgery or a nameless face.

I chose Froedtert & the Medical College because, to me, my emotional comfort was just as important as my physical wellness. I needed to know that the surgical oncologist was looking at my situation with the same fighting spirit against my cancer as I was. My surgical oncologist made me feel 100 percent confident that she was out to destroy my cancer and was going to cure it. She took the time to answer all of our questions. She scheduled my surgery based on the urgency of my condition, not on her availability. I felt as if I was her number one concern. It was an easy choice after I'd done a comparison of the two doctors.

She discussed my surgical plan with me and Lyle. I was happy to hear that she wanted to make sure that I would still have some semblance of normalcy with regard to my appearance. I appreciated that. That day at Froedtert & the Medical College took what seemed like hours to get through. We met my surgical oncologist, one of her nurses, and a pharmacist. They were very thorough and worked as a team, with a great deal of kindness and professionalism. They never made us feel as if our concerns didn't matter. Everyone worked hard. The care was stellar. What a comfort that was, knowing my providers actually cared about my health. It wasn't about us as patients being there for them; it was about them as providers being there for us. We weren't just known as a type of cancer; we were people with families and other loved ones who wanted to see us stick around a little bit longer. They are a blessing to all whom they serve— definitely one of our answered prayers.

Surgery was scheduled for the following week on Monday, just a few days away. My surgeon explained to us everything that was going to happen during surgery and what to expect afterward, including the fact

For God did not give us a spirit of timidity, but a
spirit of power, of love and of self-discipline.
—2 Timothy 1:7

that I would be going home with a cute little drain tube and a thirty-day supply of Lovenox. I was ready. I still had not looked up any pictures of my surgery on the Internet. I was scheduled for a right radical vulvectomy with lymph node removal on the right side, and possibly the left as well.

Social Media Post

So, I went to Froedtert today and saw a very impressive gynecological oncologist. I was a little taken aback when she told me my cancer is considered stage 4. However, surgery is scheduled for Monday … and chemo and radiation after. She is pretty positive we are going through all of this for a cure. Please continue to pray for me and my family. I am still very positive. I was blessed to have my old friend Sheryl join us at my appointment today. There are a lot of great quotes and encouraging scripture out there. My eyes are focused upward; prayer brings me much peace. I truly cannot believe how this diagnosis has changed my outlook on life. I realize just how precious it is. So, what I say to you, my friends: love even when it is difficult, smile even when frowning is easier, hug your kids often, and go that extra mile for others even when you don't think you can go any farther. Take time to always look for the beauty and good in everything. Stop, breathe, and love life. I am planning on six weeks out for surgery, and I look forward to being back at work doing just that—working. And when I am not at work, I plan on loving my family.

My friend Dr. Green had warned me not to look any images up. Until this point, I had listened to her. I wish I would have continued to heed her advice, because the pictures were much more horrific than what I ended up with. My humorous saying to describe my vulva is now the same as it is for my makeup: "Less is more." After all, you have to make the best of every situation. Besides, all of my parts function. The cancer was cut out. I am okay with that. I guess the point I am trying to make is that you shouldn't read too much into what is on the Internet. I think most of those

Therefore, if anyone is in Christ, he is a new creation;
the old has gone, the new has come!
—2 Corinthians 5:17

pictures must have been from when that procedure was first performed, before considerable advances were made. I am sure surgical styles come in to play as well. It appeared to me that in most of those images, staples were the preferred method for closing the wounds. All I can say to that is, *ouch!* My surgical oncologist used dissolvable stitches, and the surgical sites healed very nicely. You have to stay positive and care for your body. If you do that, your healing process becomes less cumbersome.

Social Media Post written by Lyle Torres, February 1, 2016

Laura's surgery went well. She is in the recovery room for a spell. … Docs are happy with the outcome. I will keep all of you posted. Thank you for your support. Still have a battle ahead, but she is a tough cookie.

Your own surgical scars won't look like anyone else's because they will be yours and we are all unique. I have not found any images that look like mine yet, which I am very thankful to God for. I am also thankful to my totally awesome surgeon and her team. I think we all look for what to expect so that we are better able to wrap our minds around it. We don't want to wonder about what to expect. Fear of the unknown is very real, especially when dealing with cancer, but I have since learned to take things one day at a time and not to look too far ahead of anything. I savor my time with the people I love. I live in the moment, making every second of each day count for something. I try to fill my days by doing kindnesses for others, because it fills my soul with joy. It is amazing how good you can feel when your focus is no longer on yourself. You actually benefit the most, I think, by being a blessing to others. It leaves you with no time to focus on or worry about what is going on with you. Don't fill yourself with stress by worrying; choose to be blessed instead. You can still find much joy amid all of the unpleasantness.

When the proconsul saw what had happened, he believed,
for he was amazed at the teaching about the Lord.
—Acts 13:12

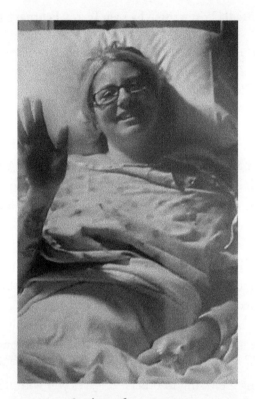

Smiling after surgery.

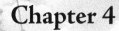

Chapter 4

Social Media Post, February 4, 2016

Hello, everyone. It has been two days since surgery. Those of you who know me, know this is torture for me to be so sedentary, lol. But for all of you wondering, yes, I am listening to the doctors and my fabulous nurse, Lyle Torres. He is taking such good care of me. God is so good. Through this storm, so far the metastatic cancer is localized and my surgery went well. Healing is rough, but I am a warrior and am keeping my chin up and my eyes on the Lord. My daughter is home from Florida to help. I had not seen her in almost two years. I have been so humbled by all of the love, prayers, and well-wishes. I can do all things through Christ, who strengthens me.

I only had to stay in the hospital one night. Being stubborn was helpful, as I didn't want to be there any longer than one night, but the fact that everything went extremely well was the deciding factor. That was an answered prayer. Surprisingly enough, there was not an extreme amount of pain, considering that a fairly large part of my body had just been cut away. The hospital staff was great. They made sure my wounds were dressed and that I knew exactly what had to be done in order to minimize the risk of infection.

The first week home was rough. When your surgical site is located where you sit, and when you have a drain tube with a grenade protruding from you abdomen, it brings new meaning to the phrase *get comfortable*. Typically, when I was finally able to relax and could snuggle into my chair, or bed, that was when I usually had to go to the bathroom. For the first two weeks or so that I was home, trips to the bathroom were a two-person

By standing firm you will gain life.
—Luke 21:19

project. Lyle took a week off work to come stay with me right after my surgery. He was a huge help. That also meant I didn't have to traumatize my daughters at that point. It was kind of hard to see what was going on with my surgical site, and it was imperative to keep it clean. I certainly didn't want to risk getting an infection. Luckily, my daughter Kayla flew in from Florida to take over after Lyle could no longer be there on a daily basis. It was a tag-team effort.

Social Media Post, February 6, 2016

I want to say thank you to everyone who has been helping, praying for, and loving me. I am so blessed. I will no doubt take friends up on offers for rides, meals, company, and errands. My ability to be still is truly being tested now. One request I have for everyone is to put your prayers into action. Help someone out today, every day. Pay a kindness forward. It might be the only light that the recipient receives in their whole day. Smile, love, laugh, pray. Look for your blessings daily and share them. God bless you all.

Social Media Post written by Brianna Rex, February 9, 2016

Guys, I don't really post a lot of stuff about raising money and stuff like that, but this is soooooo important to Roman, me, and the kids! Laura is my second mother. She is literally one of the strongest people I know, so loving and just overall an absolutely wonderful person. She really could use the help right now, between medical costs and everything else. Let's all just come together and help her kick this cancer's butt and help any way we can!

Each day things got better and better. The drain was a pain, not in the sense that it hurt, but in the sense that I kept getting tissue clogs in it, so I was constantly having to "milk" it in order to get it to suction properly. Eventually the clogs would come out, at which point the drain would start working smoothly again—until the next time. The last time it happened, it

Do not let your hearts be troubled. Trust in God, trust also in me.
—John 14:1

was a doozy. The tube was so stopped up that no fluids were getting through it. I had made it my mission to clear it. It was gross and kind of cool at the same time. Knowing that the tissues inside of the clear tube were coming from inside me was mildly disturbing, but I also found the mechanics of it all very fascinating. It took me almost thirty-six hours to work that clump of tissue through and finally get it out. I felt very accomplished. It was a victory. I know it doesn't sound like much, but every victory counts.

Social Media Post, February 10, 2016

I have to say it was great to see many of my work family when I stopped in to fill a prescription. I have tried to keep everyone updated on my current diagnosis. I did see my gynecological oncologist at Froedtert & the Medical College yesterday. The surgical site looks good and is healing well, but my drain is being stubborn. With a tissue clog, it only drains with a lot of extra work on my part … lol. Go figure. So please pray that this drain will start working like it is supposed to so I can get it out next week. Otherwise I will need to keep it in for another week after that. In the grand scheme of things, I have nothing to complain about. The doctor appointment went well—close but clear margins regarding cancer removal, which is great news. I will have to do more radiation than we thought at first, along with chemo, but that is all right with me. I recently saw a flyer for a child who is one year old, battling a rare liver cancer. Please keep this little guy in your prayers, as well as my good friend Phyllis Orth, who is battling a recurrence of ovarian cancer. There are so many other people we know who are affected by cancer. Lift them to the Lord.

I have been truly touched by all those who are coming on March 5 and to those who have gone on the GoFundMe page. In a world where it often seems as if people don't care, I have been shown how wrong I am. All I try to do is what is good and what is right, to be compassionate and caring and loving to all those around me, without expecting anything in return. So for so many people to be

Consider it pure joy, my brothers, whenever you face trials of many kinds, because you know the testing of your faith develops perseverance.
—James 1:2–3

there for me right now—I am overwhelmed … continuously. I cannot express how thankful I am to everyone. God bless you all.

I only had to keep the drain for a few weeks. During that time, I used it as a teaching tool for my granddaughter, Lily. I showed her Geema's "grenade." She was so sweet. She touched the tubing and inspected the receptacle with its fluid collection. She would look up at me and say, "Oh, Geema," with such empathy in her voice, and with concern on her little face. "It's okay. You are going to be okay." She understood, without understanding cancer, that her geema was sick, and that is all she needed to know.

Having fun with my drain.

***Make every effort to live in peace with all men and to be
holy; without holiness, no one will see the Lord.
—Hebrews 12:14***

Every time I would see Lily, she would look for any visible signs of new "owies" and tell me that I was going to be all right. She was always my sweet ray of sunshine, my little Lily Bean. Don't think the little ones in your life won't understand when something isn't right. They know, and they need to know something so they can understand why they might not see you as much, or why you may not be able to play with them or pick them up. They will understand. They get it. They do understand when things are not the same. You will be amazed by how their little brains work, and when you see the compassion and love in their eyes, it will still your heart. I didn't have to sit down and explain cancer to Lily; I just told her that geema didn't feel well and that she had a big owie. Lily knew that if there were new Band-Aids, there were new owies. She was very careful with her geema. If I was having a bad day, she, at two and a half years old, would sit in my chair with me, hold my hand, and not move for hours. Simply amazing.

Social Media Post, February 16, 2016

Off to the doctor this afternoon. Praying the drain tube comes out today. I seem to be healing up well, so we will see what they say. I am feeling all right, other than being super sore and not having much of an appetite. Enjoying time with my daughter who is here from Florida. Wish she could stay longer. Heads-up for March 5. I know many of you know, but my best friend, Marcy Prochnow, is putting together a benefit to help with mounting medical bills (they waste no time getting those mailed out). It will be at the VFW from 2:00 to 7:00. I have been amazed by the outpouring of support, all of the donations for raffles, and the donations of food. I am truly looking forward to spending time with friends and family that day. It is a blessing. Marcy has been working so hard to make this event a successful one. I cannot believe the generosity of so many. So emotionally overwhelming. I just want to continue to say thank you and God bless you all. Please continue to keep praying for all those in need. Your prayers do not go unheard.

Chapter 5

My follow-up visit for wound care and a drain check came and went. The drain tube was to stay put for another week. Boo. That is the best G-rated word I could find to describe how I felt about that. It wasn't even that it bothered me anymore. It wasn't painful. It didn't really get in the way. I had become quite used to its being there, but it was that fact alone that was frustrating. It was still there. So I did what most people do when they get news they don't want to hear: I complained about it for a minute, and then I moved on. The drain removal became another countdown for me to look forward to. I could do seven more days: piece of cake.

Once I hit week four postsurgery, I was able to sit without my trusted boppy pillow under my rear. The boppy pillow is the best invention since sliced bread, in my opinion. I highly recommend it for anyone going through any type of surgery involving your seating area. It was certainly not made just for babies; however, babies look much cuter in them. It was so much more comfortable than a blow-up pillow, although those do work in a pinch. I also discovered that just taking a blanket and rolling it into a circle works well for long car rides, because you are able to adjust that even more than the boppy.

Week four included a great milestone. I no longer needed assistance in the bathroom, which gave me a little bit of my dignity back and allowed my daughters the chance to scrub their brains of any traumatic imagery. I do have to say, they handled all of it pretty well, especially my youngest, Celese. I think that all of the care I received from Lyle, my daughters, and even my best friend was more awkward for me than for my caregivers, especially my girls. I am the mom, and it almost felt like the roles were reversed. I am way too young for all of that. I was wishing to save the diaper jokes for when I was a little older, but as you probably know, when

But I trust in your unfailing love; my heart rejoices in your salvation. I will sing to the Lord, for He has been good to me.
—Psalm 13:5–6

your family loves you, they can't resist—and laughter is still the best medicine sometimes.

Social Media Post, March 1, 2016

The first of three doctor's appointments this week is later today. It always snows, of course. But the snow is beautiful. I am pretty sure chemo and radiation start next week. Probably will get a port placed this week. So far, so good. Anyone who knows me, knows it takes a lot to get me down. I am an overachiever, so I figure that applies to cancer as well, lol. I am sad that my daughter Kayla Arneson had to go back home, but I was blessed with having her here for a few weeks to help with my surgical recovery (and adding to the number of people yelling at me not to do things, lol). God is good. I will keep everyone updated. Totally looking forward to this Saturday when I can see everyone. I feel as if I have spent the last four weeks on the couch, lol. Remember, everyone, smile even when you don't want to; it might be someone else's blessing. Have a great Tuesday.

Social Media Post, March 2, 2016

Well, the doctor's appointment went well yesterday. All surgical sites are healing beautifully. I do have to concentrate on walking without favoring my right side, because it is causing a certain amount of hip pain, but this should pass. I see the radiation oncologist Friday. Going to continue treatments at Froedtert & the Medical College because they have been excellent every step of the way. We will see if I get a PICC line or a port. Chemo and radiation are starting in two weeks. They want me to be a little more healed up first. So there have been a lot of answered prayers and a lot to be thankful for. God is good.

The original plan was to do six weeks of radiation and chemotherapy.

> *I tell you the truth, whoever hears my words and believes him who sent me has eternal life, and will not be condemned; he has crossed over from death to life.*
> *—John 5:24–25*

I was elated when my health-care providers changed it from six weeks to five weeks of treatment. My port placement was scheduled as well. I was probably more nervous about that, more than any other part of my treatment plan. I'm not sure why, other than the fact that I would be awake for the procedure and it was my understanding that they would be ramming a tube into the vein in my neck and implanting a device into my chest. It didn't sound pleasant. The fear of the unknown; that was huge throughout this journey. The day before I was scheduled to have my port placed, I watched an episode of a popular medical drama on television. This particular episode depicted a patient coming in to the emergency department. In the end, she died from an infected port site during the port removal. ***Of course she died!*** That only added to my anxiety. That, coupled with the personal experience of one of my friends who developed a large clot under her port after it was placed. Needless to say, I did not sleep well the night before my procedure. The day off was filled with continual prayer, which did keep the anxiety at bay.

Social Media Post, March 17, 2016

Well, tomorrow is the big day for my port placement. It is funny how major surgery was no big deal to me, but this is a little unnerving. I imagine it is because I will have this thing under my skin for the next six or seven weeks, snaked up into my neck. Sounds like big fun, eh? I know, I know … I can do it, lol. Please pray it all goes well and there are no complications. Radiation starts Monday too, and that puts me one day closer to curing this cancer. I was warned about how supportive my work (employer) would be through this. By work, I mean HR, because I work with the best, most caring people in the world. I got my first letter stating my continuous leave is not approved and my job is not protected. Like I want to worry about that right now too. Please pray that

Finally, brothers, whatever is true, whatever is noble, whatever is right, whatever is pure, whatever is lovely, whatever is admirable— if anything is excellent or praiseworthy—think about such things. Whatever you have learned or received or heard from me, or seen in me—put into practice. And the God of peace will be with you. —Philippians 4:8–9

this next set of forms I take to the doctor to be filled out takes care of the HR department, although I know God has a plan for me. I love you all and miss everyone. Since I don't get out much, if there is anyone I can be praying for, please private-message me, because I would love to pray for you and your needs.

Lyle was a godsend in the surgical services area while I waited to be taken back for my procedure. He kept talking with me, praying with me, and letting me know everything was going to be all right, even if that meant answering the same questions for me over and over again. The nursing staff had offered me medication for the anxiety, but I'd turned it down. I really didn't care for the way that medication made me feel.

The interventional radiology team was running behind that day, by a few hours, because of emergencies, so our wait time in the pre-procedure area was longer than normal. But they did everything they could to make us comfortable. This didn't help my anxiety at all. I was my worst enemy. When I was finally wheeled away, the peace of the Lord fell over me like a blanket, and I was reminded, as I lay on the gurney in the hallway outside the procedure room, that I was not alone. My fears were not completely washed away, but it was like holding on to my best friend's hand. It was all right, because I knew that no matter what, He was there.

Everything went as planned. I discovered that the time I'd spent worrying was a complete waste. The only pain I felt was the stick, sting, and burn from the administration of the local anesthetic, no worse than getting stitches. Apart from that, I felt a little tugging and pulling, but no pain. I was able to have a conversation with the staff throughout the entire procedure, which only took about thirty minutes. When they were finished, they glued me back together and then placed Steri-Strips across the incision. I was taken to my room and given aftercare instructions to follow. I only had a short wait after that, before I was able to head home. I healed from the port placement with no complications. It did feel strange to have this foreign object lodged in my neck like an octopus, but eventually I got used to it.

Thanks be to God for his indescribable gift!
—2 Corinthians 9:15

Social Media Post, March 18, 2016

Port placement went well. Long day. They were running almost three hours behind due to multiple emergencies, but they were fabulous. Neck is soooo sore, but this too shall pass. Thank you so much for all your prayers. Next stop, chemo and radiation. It is an interesting journey.

The Lord is my rock, my fortress and my deliverer, my God is my rock, in whom I take refuge. He is my shield and the horn of my salvation, my stronghold.
—Psalm 18:2

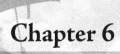

Chapter 6

Social Media Post, March 4, 2016

Doctor appointment went well today. I have my radiation-planning CT scan on Monday, and chemo and radiation should begin in approximately two weeks. I will need both for five to six weeks. Going for a backward bikini-line sunburn … ouch. Went over all side effects as well, again, and all I can say is, we will take this one day at a time. We are praying for the treatment to be a cure, so I will go through it with a thankful heart, because my desire is to be here for my family, because I love them so much. I hope to see many of you tomorrow. There will be food and over sixty baskets to raffle off! I again have to say how humbled I am by everyone's kindness and generosity. God is good.

I think everyone has the nightmare where they are planning a big event and no one shows up. I remember thinking how sad it would be if no one came to the benefit. Fortunately, that was not the case. The VFW was flooded with friends and family. There were people whom I didn't know who came and gave just because they wanted to support the cause. I was stunned.

Social Media Post, March 6, 2016

Very tired and sore, but I have to say thank you to everyone who has been so supportive of me through well-wishes, prayers, visits, and donations. The fund-raiser was a huge success. I cannot believe how large the turnout was. I had a nightmare Friday night that no

No one will be able to stand up against you all the days of your life. As I was with Moses, so I will be with you: I will never leave you nor forsake you.
—Joshua 1:5

one came, lol. Everyone came in support. I guess you don't realize how many lives you touch until you are the one in need. I love you all so much, and even though I am exhausted, I loved seeing everyone. Please continue to pray. Next up, six weeks of chemo and radiation. God is good. Through Him all things are possible.

The fund-raiser was amazing. We did have an issue with someone stealing, but that was a minor hiccup in the grand scheme of things. Everyone's generosity was overwhelming to me. So many people came to help. I couldn't believe how tiring just sitting there was for me. I felt helpless, and a little funny about having people fussing over me. I was usually the one doing the fussing, taking care of others. I was not used to being on the receiving end of it. It made me a little uncomfortable at first.

With the money that was raised, I was able to remit larger payments toward my continuously growing medical bills, pay my rent ahead a few months, and ensure my kids would be taken care of in the process of this whole mess. Cancer invades every aspect of your life. The benefit was a huge blessing to me and my family.

Me and my twins, Grace and Celese, at the fund-raiser one month after my surgery.

***Now faith is being sure of what we hope for
and certain of what we do not see.
—Hebrews 11:1***

Social Media Post, March 10, 2016

I am in the process of sending out thank-you cards, but I just want to say thank you again, to all my family, my friends, and even people who don't know me, who have been supportive and have been praying. It means so much to me. I found out I will be out of work a little longer than I had anticipated. Radiation sounds like a real treat. Please keep praying. God bless you.

Chapter 7

Social Media Post, March 21, 2016

My port area is a little sore, but it is nicely healed. Praise the Lord. First radiation treatment today, then only twenty-nine more to go. I get to have the weekends off. Lol. This will be the most expensive sunburn and bikini wax ever! Lol. But my mind is at peace amid all of the storms raging in my life right now. I do not like to air my personal laundry on social media, so I will just ask for prayers for my family and continued prayers for my health. So many prayer warriors out there. God is good, all the time, and I know we are always right where we are supposed to be any particular moment. I would like to give a huge shout of thanks to my BFF, Marcy Prochnow, for all of her support and everything she has done to ensure I am taken care of. I would also like to thank everyone who brought meals. What a blessing. I truly am blessed to be loved by so many awesome people. I will post updates, to keep everyone in the loop. God bless you all. Happy Monday!

My first chemotherapy treatment was on a Tuesday, four days after my port placement. It was definitely a long day, as my treatments took five hours each time I went, and then I still had to go to radiation afterward. All of that was followed up by a doctor's appointment at the very end of the day. Lyle and I usually spent a good eight hours at Froedtert & the Medical College on Tuesdays. It was an all-day event filled with poking, jabbing, and baking, but it was also filled with jokes and laughter. The rest of the week always went by fairly quickly. It took longer to drive to the hospital on radiation days than it did to receive the treatments. I was lucky to have

O my Strength, I sing praise to you; you O God,
are my fortress, my loving God.
—Psalm 59:17

multiple people volunteer to take me up there and drive me back. I would have never been able to drive myself.

Lyle was always my guy Tuesday. I was thankful for that, since Tuesdays were long. I think he wanted to be there, not only because of that, but also because he wanted to make sure everything went well. My first treatment went smoothly. It was perfect. There were no problems accessing my port, nothing was painful, and the infusion didn't make me feel any different. It was like I was soaking up an IV filled with saline, not the toxic cocktail I knew was pumping through my body. It was just time-consuming.

I was always setting little goals for myself. Some of them bordered on ridiculous, but it was the little things that helped pass the time. For the first three days following chemotherapy, your urine is considered "radioactive," so you have to wipe down the toilet and make sure you flush it twice after use if you are using the facilities at home. While at my treatments, I had to use an assigned restrooms, with the proper measuring supplies in them, as I had to measure my urine output during the treatment processes. Other chemo patients had to do the same. The staff had to ensure that we were properly hydrated, and that what went in came out. The more output, the better. I kept track on a dry-erase board in my room, continually trying to beat my previous score. The nurses were happy with my numbers, and I was playing an amusing game with myself. It was a win-win situation. I was especially happy with this, because even hitting the toilet at that point in the game was still very difficult. That was because of the surgery, though, not the chemo.

Social Media Post, March 24, 2016

So far, so good. One chemo treatment done with no major hitches, and so far, radiation treatments are on point. I am feeling a little tired and not quite myself, but anyone who knows me, knows I am still trying to push through things. God is good, and I know He will carry me through this. My prayers continue to be said for those I

Test me, O Lord, and try me, examine my heart and my mind, for your love is ever before me, and I walk continually in your truth.
—Psalm 26:2–3

know are struggling in their lives. If you have any special requests, give me a shout. I miss working and my family.

Social Media Post, March 25, 2016

Last day of radiation for the week, whoop, whoop. Then I get two days where I am not being pumped full of toxic chemicals or microwaved. Lol. Ha-ha. The song "Radioactive" was playing during my last treatment. I found it funny—ironic, but funny. So today will conclude week one. Praise the Lord. Happy Friday, everyone! Love and miss all of you! Have a great weekend.

The technicians in the radiation department were fabulous. I loved getting to know everyone there. I was never cared for by a mean-spirited person, even when it seemed as if certain staff members were having a bad day. Their friendliness always made being there less traumatic and more comforting, even when what I was going through wasn't particularly comfortable. Many of the women working there were pregnant. Being able to talk with them about babies and their families created a more personal environment. Exchanging stories with each other made it more of a friendship than a medical professional–patient relationship. I looked forward to talking with them when I went in. I loved sharing my experiences with my own children and hearing about theirs. The girls were always making sure I was comfortable and feeling all right to proceed. We counted down the days of treatment together. Finishing up with radiation was one more goal I looked forward to reaching.

It is God who arms me with strength and makes my way perfect.
—Psalm 18:32

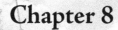

Chapter 8

Social Media Post, March 30, 2016

Second chemo treatment down. Had a nice comfy room this time; did a lot of cross-stitching and reflecting. No complications. That is always good. Lyle is now singing "Poison" ("That girl is poison …"), as he'll be doing for the next two days. Gotta have humor in all of this. It is very important. I am in the middle of the second week of radiation. No noticeable skin changes yet, but I feel pretty equivalent to the desert, so I am sure they are coming. That is probably what I am looking forward to the least, but this too shall pass. I would like to again thank everyone for their prayers and well-wishes. The cards, the calls—they seem to always come at just the right time. God bless you all.

All of my appointments for chemotherapy between my second round and my last round came with only a minor complication. I had clots in my port, which, as I understand it, are fairly common. The staff had to administer a medication called TPA (tissue plasminogen activator, a clot buster) in order to break up the clot, before they could access my port. This wasn't painful, but it did tack an extra hour onto my already long and tedious chemotherapy appointment. Having the TPA administered was something I just kind of got used to. The first time I had to have it, I can honestly say I was a little nervous. I had only heard of TPA being used with stroke patients, and from what I understood about it (which wasn't much), it can have disastrous consequences. For me, the administration went smoothly. After waiting forty-five to fifty minutes, the staff were able to access my port, and then my treatment went on as usual.

> ***Jesus replied: "Love the Lord your God with all your heart and with all your soul and with all you mind."***
> ***—Matthew 22:37***

I think that with cancer, the unknown is the scariest part. You want to know if you are going to get sick after they give you medicine, or if the procedures they will be doing are going to be painful. Each and every day can bring you a new challenge. I know God does not make bad things happen to people, but He does allow them to happen, in order to reveal His glory. Even with God by my side each and every step of the way, I can honestly say that new procedures and new diagnoses still frightened me, but they frightened me in a different way. I wasn't afraid to die, because I knew there was a room prepared for me in heaven. I knew I had salvation through my Lord Jesus Christ, and I took comfort in that, but I still feared the pain and sickness. Nobody wants to be miserable. Nobody wants to be in pain, and more than being sick, I feared not having enough time to reach out to my children with God's Word before being called home. I had wasted so much time already. I now faced the reality that my time might run out.

Before my body became ill, I didn't realize how inconsistent my walk with Jesus was. It is funny how, when we are faced with a life-and-death struggle, the gray lines disappear and things really do become crystal clear. Moral convictions really do become something you own, believe in, and defend. When you are living with cancer, you know in an instant how serious the battle for your soul is. After all, eternity is never ending. This life is only a temporary pit stop along the way. We are not in control, nothing ever goes according to our plans, no matter how hard we try to maintain control. I know that things certainly did not go according to my plan, and I am taking a guess that they haven't for most, no matter what people are struggling with. For some it will be cancer. Others will have emotional or spiritual battles, and still others will have physical struggles that leave them vulnerable and weak. God has the master plan for all of us. Trust in the Lord with all of your heart, not just some of it. Don't waste a single second of your life. Love your family, love your friends, love your enemies, and love yourself. Do not spend time being hateful,

I have told you these things, so that in me you may have peace. In this world, you will have trouble. But take heart! I have overcome the world.
—John 16:33

jealous, or prideful. These things are not of God and will surely destroy you. In all things, love. It is very important as you go through treatment to rid yourself of negativity. It really does change everything. Look for your blessings daily, and eventually that is all you will see.

Chapter 9

Social Media Post, April 1, 2016

Well, my second week of treatments is coming to an end. I have my last radiation treatment at noon. My skin remains intact so far; it just looks a little sunburned. I am trying to push through the fatigue and nausea. All this lying around drives me crazy. My son David Salas has some of his artwork showing tonight at a local gallery. I am very proud of him. So I am saving my oomph for that. Please keep praying. God works miracles in my life every day, blessing every moment. I want to give a shout-out, to praise the Lord through this storm. I love you, my friends. Keeping the faith.

I had a welcome distraction from all things cancer related, when my son was chosen, to have his artwork displayed at a local downtown gallery. The show was successful. There were many talented young artists there, my son being one of them. He is so artistically talented. I enjoy it every time he shows his artwork to me. My ex-husband, David Salas, and his girlfriend Lisa came to the gallery that night as well. Afterward, we all went to a local downtown restaurant together and got something to eat. It was a great night spent with family and friends. I even lived dangerously and took off my face mask for a while. I have to say, it can be rather claustrophobic wearing those all the time, not to mention that my glasses always fogged up when I wore mine. I only kept it off for a little while. It was good to feel as if everything was back to normal, even if it was only for a little while. The laughter we shared was great medicine and I savored every moment.

Saturday and Sunday were difficult because I wanted to feel better

Therefore, I tell you, whatever you ask for in prayer, believe that you have received it, and it will be yours.
—Mark 11:24

while my Lyle was in town, but I was starting to feel more and more of the side effects from chemotherapy and radiation. The heartburn and the metal taste in my mouth were the most annoying of all, followed closely by the never-ending feeling of being drained.

Even with the side effects, I still managed to enjoy the little things such as playing a game of backgammon, watching movies with my family, going to church, and laughing with my family and friends. I still missed work terribly, along with all my coworkers and patients, who had become, in a sense, a second family to me.

Social Media Post, April 4, 2016

And we are off. Here comes week three. I am starting to feel all the lovely side effects, including neuropathy in my hands and feet, fatigue, ringing in my ears, and severe heartburn, not to mention that with all the radiation, simply using the bathroom is not pleasant. I know, too much information, lol. I have two requests: One, pray. Without God, I would not be in the frame of mind I am today. God is good, and I am truly blessed every day. Two, consider making a donation of fake flowers. I would like to keep myself occupied by creating floral arrangements for our nursing home residents who may not have any beautiful things brought to them. So if you have old fake floral arrangements sitting around or anything I can use to do this, shoot me a message. It would certainly bless others. Have a great Monday, and God bless you.

Keeping myself occupied throughout my treatment was a struggle at times. What do you do with yourself all day when you don't even want to get up to go to the bathroom, or you can no longer walk well enough on your own without falling into things? The neuropathy in my hands was transient, disappearing as quickly as it had arrived. I was very thankful for that, because I do so much to pass the time that requires the use of my hands. One of my favorite ways to pass the time was to cross-stitch. Being able to use and feel one's fingertips is very important to be able to cross-stitch. Even when the neuropathy did make my fingertips numb and tingly, I stitched anyway. I just had to be careful not to bleed on anything after I poked myself, which was often.

I was almost halfway done with treatments and it was still not horrible.

I could manage, but I knew that I wouldn't be able to much longer. I watched how other women who were receiving the same radiation walked when they came out of treatment. I knew it was going to get much worse before it was going to get better. I had to tell myself I was like the little engine that could, only instead of saying, "I think I can," I was saying, "I know I can with Christ, who strengthens me." If I had to suffer, so be it. It was going to be the equivalent of a paper cut when compared to what Christ endured. I never wasted any time feeling sorry for myself. For a fleeting moment in the beginning, I asked "Why me?" but really, why not me? If it turned out that things didn't work out for me, I would still be at peace. Sure, I wanted to live longer and see my children all grown up and doing great things with their lives. I wanted to see them eventually get married and have families of their own. We all want that for ourselves, don't we? I thought about the life that I'd had so far. I'd been married. I had children. I enjoyed being able to nurture them and watch them grow. I had a great best friend and had the pleasure of having the best work family anyone could have. I'd served in the army reserves. I'd earned a college degree. As I reflected on my life, I realized how many life experiences I had already tasted. I felt selfish for wanting more, especially when there were so many children battling illnesses who would not get to experience any of the things that I'd experienced. Opening my eyes to this reality made me even more thankful and grateful for everything I'd had and done, even my cancer. Cancer had opened my eyes and allowed my faith to grow in ways I did not think were possible. It had brought me to a place of great joy and peace. It can bring these things to you as well.

What do you place your hope in? There will come a point in your life when you will face death. We can't escape that. Death is inevitable. Faith is, after all, believing in what you cannot see. I am here, by the grace of God, to tell you that throughout my treatments, I was never alone. I was filled with a peace that surpasses my comprehension. Even when life has you turned upside down—and believe me, my life had been doing handstands—peace and comfort can be with you daily. You too can have

Then Jesus declared, "I am the bread of life. He who comes to me will
never do hungry, and he who believes in me will never be thirsty."
—John 6:35

this peace in Christ Jesus. I can't sugarcoat it. I can only share my experiences. Cancer is not the only struggle people face. There is a war being waged for our souls, and it is important for you to know that you do not ever have to go into battle alone.

Give thanks in all circumstances.
—1 Thessalonians 5:18

Chapter 10

The third week of my treatment was complete. With the extra hour being tacked on for TPA prior to chemotherapy, Tuesday was still a long treatment day. Lyle and I spent it watching movies, while I cross-stitched. I had to have something to do with my hands while I was lying there in that bed or sitting in the chair, something other than just being a patient with cancer. I enjoyed talking with the nurses, all of whom were very nice. I was also still trying to beat the previous week's urine output score. Lyle and I were the fun room, and I was the fun patient to take care of. We were always being silly. I figured the nurses' job was hard enough on a daily basis without having more unpleasant, negative patients to take care of. Even when I didn't feel the greatest, it never hurt my face to smile. And it was always just as easy to be nice as it would have been to be nasty.

Kicking back and enjoying chemotherapy.

We live by faith, not by sight.
—2 Corinthians 5:7

Social Media Post, April 6, 2016

Gotta love steroids. They will keep you up for days, lol. My third round of chemo went off with just a little hiccup. There was a blood clot in my port, so I had to be injected with TPA in order to dissolve the clot. Once we got that done and it worked, praise the Lord, chemo flowed freely, giving me yet another beautiful Oompa Loompa glow. So today is the halfway marker for treatment, and according to all of my fabulous docs, treatment is going according to plan, and the plan is to cure. I like the plan. Please keep praying that this remains God's plan as well. I feel as if there is so much to do still, with my eyes wide open this time. So many people in need. Everyone can do their part—kind words, polite gestures, a smile. Loving really is easier than hating, as sappy as that sounds. God bless you. Have an awesome Wednesday!

Radiation was still going good. Walking was getting a little more difficult. I could see that the radiation technicians who took care of me on a daily basis were now watching how I was walking and always asking me how I was feeling. No matter how I felt, I always loved our chats. I enjoyed sharing with them. I even brought in some recipes for them to try. I love to cook, so we often talked about food. Kids and food. Those were the main topics. Food had become an even greater obsession for me while I was going through treatments. I binge-watched every cooking show I could find. I found it funny, because at the time, nothing tasted good to me, but that certainly didn't stop food from looking good to me. Mental torture? I don't know. But I sucked my kids and my boyfriend into watching the shows with me. Soon we were all addicted.

Social Media Post, April 8, 2016

Well, week three is coming to an end today. Yahoo. Only two more weeks and a day left to go. Praise the Lord! Have a great Friday.

**For we know that our old self was crucified with him so that the body of sin might be done away with, that we should no longer be slaves to sin—because anyone who has died has been freed from sin.
—Romans 6:6–7**

Remember to pay forward what you can—a smile, a kindness. It really does bless others. Have a great weekend, everyone!

The end of week three. Thank the Lord, I had only two weeks to go. And now I had two days off where I didn't have to go into the microwave. I wanted to believe that in those two days, all the damage that had been done by that enormous machine would be undone, and then it would be like starting over on the following Monday. I was going to be the one who didn't have any awful skin reactions. Many of us want to feel as if we can go through things like a superhero. I wanted to believe I could remain unscathed by the radioactive waves that were cooking me from the inside out.

My weekends were bittersweet. On the one hand, I got to spend them with Lyle. On the other hand, as my treatments progressed, the heartburn got worse, and Saturday, Sunday, and Monday were usually when things flared to the point of being almost unbearable.

Social Media Post, April 11, 2016

First day of week four done. Tomorrow is my fourth chemo treatment, with one left, hopefully, after that. Getting pretty uncomfortable, but my eyes are to the sky. God is good all the time. So far treatments are going according to plan, and a cure is still the goal. The heartburn is still awful—unbearable at times— and balancing my diet has been difficult but doable. In the grand scheme of things, I have nothing to complain about and everything to be thankful for. I want to say thank you for continued cards, well-wishes, and prayers. It means a lot to me and my family.

I was very glad I had only two more chemotherapy treatments to do. I prayed that it would not take long for the effects of the chemo to fade from my body after I'd completed all my scheduled treatments. I could not even imagine doing this for months, like others do. I know all treatments differ,

For God is not a God of disorder, but of peace.
—1 Corinthians 14:33

and they all come with their own set of side effects, but dealing with the heartburn definitely moved to the top of my prayer list.

There were times when it got so bad that the only way I could describe it to my health-care team was to tell them it made me feel as if there was nothing more I could do to make the heartburn stop other than to jump off a building. Now I would never jump off a building, but I wanted them to know just how serious it felt to me. I was put on a few different PPIs (proton pump inhibitors), which would bring minimal relief. It wasn't until my health-care providers started me on the highest dose available for one of the meds that I actually got some relief. It was a dosage they usually gave to patients for bleeding ulcers, and of course my insurance company had an issue with that, because I was not being treated for what the dose was indicated for. By then, I was willing to pay for the medicine out of my already empty pockets to get some relief from the symptoms. My insurance did finally cover it, after my doctor's office jumped through the prior authorization hoops. It did become an ongoing struggle with my insurer, though.

Social Media Post, April 13, 2016

More TPA for my clotty port yesterday, but the good news is, only one more chemo treatment left! Yay! (Then I will respectfully insist this octopus in my neck be removed.) Nine radiation treatments left and counting, literally. Docs changed heartburn meds, so we will see how that goes. I am sure the heartburn is just from the treatments and will get better when they are over. Doc says everything is still going as scheduled, and that is good news to my ears. Please pray for continued healing and cancer obliteration (lol), not only for me, but also for all others. I also have a little prayer request: pray for God's provision to continue to see us through, and for an unspoken request that God is well aware of, as it weighs heavily on my heart. Keeping the faith, my friends. God is good all the time. Happy Wednesday!

Therefore, my dear brothers, stand firm. Let nothing move you.
Always give yourselves fully to the work of the Lord, because
you know that your labor in the Lord is not in vain.
—1 Corinthians 15:58

We just planned for extra-long chemo days. I enjoyed them, though. Lyle learned his way around the hospital and the clinics, which was good, because I often sent him on adventures to find something for me. He always obliged my requests. Just having him there, even in silence, was a blessing to me. When he did venture out, he would always try to find an assortment of things that might taste good to me. Sadly, everything tasted like a mouthful of rusty metal. It actually turned my stomach to eat. The only thing that I could still manage to choke down was greasy cheeseburgers, but even those were beginning to leave a terribly bad aftertaste. No matter what I tried to get rid of it—gum, candy, certain mouthwashes—the horrid taste in my mouth was always there. Food just intensified it. Eating was now becoming something I had to push myself to do in order to keep my strength up.

Social Media Post, April 15, 2016

(I want to thank Lyle for reposting this.)

I have a newfound understanding of the stressors that go along with a cancer diagnosis. It changes the outlook of what is really important in your life, while at the same time turning your life completely upside down. You deal with exhaustion, physical pain, emotional ups and downs, financial burdens, job security problems, and lovely insurance battles, just to name a few. Life zooms in around you, and you feel like you are stuck in the mud, at a standstill, fighting to pull your feet out and move forward. I am blessed though, daily. I am so thankful for the love and support we have received from everyone. The outpouring of prayers has been a godsend. My faith in Christ is stronger than ever, and I know that through this, He has a plan for all of us. Please continue to pray not only for our family, but also for others who are fighting the same battle. A lot of times it seems like when it rains, it pours, but God is good through it all, because He gives us eyes to see the

**Be very careful, then, how you live—not as unwise but as wise,
making the most of every opportunity, because the days are evil.
—Ephesians 5:15–16**

blessings through the storm. Please share this if you can, and may God bless you all.

At the end of week four, I found myself searching for a ride. I had the best ride calendar laid out, but things do happen to throw a monkey wrench into our plans. On Mondays, my mom and my brother alternated coming to town to take me to treatments. Lyle took me every Tuesday. My son Ryann took me every Wednesday. My friend Sheryl took me on Thursdays and some Fridays, and my best friend, Marcy, took me some Fridays. Sometimes the days didn't work out because people got sick. No one wants to be around the person with cancer when they are hacking and sneezing and are feverish. For the most part, I rarely had to look for a ride. When plans did fall through, there were always people who stepped right up to fill in.

Social Media Post, April 15, 2016

Still looking for a ride today. Everyone is getting sick, and no one wants to be around me when they are ill, lol. I need to be at Froedtert & the MCW [the Medical College of Wisconsin] by 2:30. Treatment takes about half an hour. Please IM me if you are able. Thank you.

My son Ryann was able to change his work schedule to take me a few times, in a pinch. His employer was very understanding and flexible. Each ride there and back was a blessing. It was time I got to spend without the distraction of the television or the Internet, just talking with whomever was taking me that day. My friend Sheryl introduced me to a great burger place on Seventy-Sixth Street in Milwaukee. I looked forward to splitting a double cheeseburger with her and having a chocolate malt every time she took me for my treatments. Finding new and delicious food experiences was a small bit of fun for us, especially when we found things that tasted good to me, even if it only lasted for a moment. By week four, I was

Then Jesus told him, "Because you have seen me, you have believed;
blessed are those who have not seen and yet have believed."
—John 20:29

also hauling the boppy pillow around with me. It had become my fifth appendage. I didn't go anywhere without it.

People looked, but I didn't care; at least I could sit with some comfort. After all, they didn't know the things I was dealing with. The experience made me realize how often I didn't know what others were going through. How quickly I would sometimes come to a conclusion that I should have never come to in the first place. Having cancer and using my boppy pillow in public changed my perspective on things a lot. How quickly we can assume we know what is going on with another human being. We think that we know what is best for them without even knowing them. I still do this at times, but now I am more aware of it than ever. My awareness helps me to guard my mouth and my mind.

Let love and faithfulness never leave you; bind them around your neck, write them on the table of your heart. Then you will win favor and a good name in the sight of God and man.
—Proverbs 3:3–4

Chapter 11

Social Media Post, April 16, 2016

Week four done. Whew. Skin is ugly. Walking funny again. I just laugh, 'cause what is the alternative? Please keep praying. One more chemo treatment next week and six more radiation treatments left. Then, I pray, I will be done with treatments and on my way to healing up. My new prayers are that no infections set in and that my endurance through this remains strong. Keep the faith, everyone.

The completion of week four was joyful. I was one week closer to putting this behind me. I had passed the halfway point. Praise the Lord! My skin was not holding up too well at this juncture. It was actually starting to resemble plastic after it has been in the microwave for too long. Great visual, isn't it? My radiation oncologist told me that the vaginal and rectal area is the worst place for radiation treatments. I didn't have anything to compare my skin problems to, but I was fairly confident that she was correct on that one. I had to chalk it up to number one in my book of horrible experiences, although, as awful as it seemed at that time, it wasn't unbearable. I was still able to smile and laugh, trying to make the best of it.

After a much-needed rest over the weekend from that devilish radiation machine, I arrived Monday to receive some bad news. I was wrong about the number of treatments I had left. I had been certain that today was the day, the last day. I was wrong. Wednesday was going to be the last day. It added only two more days, but to be honest, it made me more than a little sad.

All scripture is God-breathed and is useful for teaching, rebuking,
correcting and training in righteousness, so that the man of
God may be thoroughly equipped for every good work.
—2 Timothy 3:16–17

45

My body was wearing down rapidly, rotting from the inside out, and I was trying really hard not to let it bring my spirits down as well. What could I do? I made a joke, felt sorry for myself for like five minutes, and moved on.

Tuesday was my final chemotherapy treatment. That was a sure thing. It was a milestone to celebrate. There would be no more long Tuesdays or turning green, and eventually there would be no more metallic taste in my mouth. I looked forward to that fading away quickly. I missed the taste of food. Eating had become something I had to force myself to do, because nothing tasted good anymore. Steak, vegetables, cereal, and even a piece of hard candy all tasted the same, like metal soaked in someone's nasty saliva. The end of chemo began my new countdown. I counted the days until I could taste my food.

Social Media Post, April 19, 2016

Last chemo done. Have my lovely puke-green glow. Definitely not Maybelline, lol. Seven more radiation treatments. I am now having my skin nursed daily, and I have to sit on ice. Still, I cannot complain. Please continue to pray for all of the people battling cancer. I talk to so many every day. Everyone is affected by it somehow. But God is good, all the time. And cancer survivors are strong. Love you all. Keep the faith.

The good news is that I didn't even need TPA for my last round of chemo. We looked at that as a small victory, which we gladly accepted with a prayer of thanks. Before we left the same-day treatment floor, where we'd arrived every Tuesday, my nurse presented me with a certificate of completion that had been signed by all the nursing staff. They also gave me a cupcake. Even though that cupcake tasted like sheetrock, it was the most delicious cupcake I have ever eaten. It signified the completion of

For I was hungry and you gave me something to eat, I was thirsty and you gave me something to drink, I was a stranger and you invited me in. I needed clothes and you clothed me, I was sick and you looked after me, I was in prison and you came to visit me.
—Matthew 25:35–36

one more portion of my treatment plan. I still had to finish my radiation course, but my chapter on chemotherapy had now been closed.

The nonchalant attitude with which I had strolled in to radiation treatments for the first couple of weeks was now gone. It was difficult to walk. I became winded and tired very easily, and I lost my balance within the blink of an eye. I also had issues with incontinence now, I think, in part, because so much was now exposed thanks to the surgery, and because the radiation was really beating me up worse on the inside than it was on the outside.

As week five started, I began to notice the stench of burnt flesh. It was awful, and it took a lot for me not to let my mind dwell on what was happening to me. It became increasingly difficult to remain positive when I knew that the smell of necrotic tissue was coming from me. It smelled of death, and it made me sick to my stomach. It was just another reminder to me that my fight was still far from over. I had to keep telling myself that the old skin would shed and some new skin would appear, that this

Blessed is the man who perseveres under trial, because
when he has stood the test, he will receive the crown of
life that God has promised to those who love him.
—James 1:12

47

was only a temporary state of being, and that with time, I would be good as new.

Social Media Post, April 22, 2016

Last radiation treatment of the week, with three more to go next week. I officially hate treatment now. In a lot of pain. Don't want to use the bathroom at all ... ever. The next few weeks are going to be a challenge. I know that through this, God is teaching me and molding me. He has never left my side. God is truly good, all the time. We don't get to pick what storms ravage our lives, but we do get to decide what path we wish to take through them. I know I can do all things through Christ, who strengthens me. I want to thank Brianna Rex for cooking meals and helping with the cleaning, and I am so thankful that my daughter Kayla Arneson is back in town to help as well. I know this has not been easy for any of my children—lots of what-ifs and whys for them. But God has a plan for me, for all of us. I truly believe if you open your heart to Him, He may not change your circumstances, but He will definitely change your outlook on them. Serve one another joyously, without expecting anything in return. Love one another without judging. Build up those you love, because the world is already trying to do its best to tear them down. Thank you so much for your continued love and prayers. I even received a fun little goodie package from Tami Hermes. It put a smile on my face. I am in the home stretch, and through all of this pain, my prognosis is still on target. Just gotta break down a little more before we can build back up. I love you all. Keep the faith. God bless you.

Remaining focused on the upcoming weeks was difficult. The healing and the transformation my body was going through were incredible. I tried to focus on the healthy me that would emerge from these horrible but necessary treatments. I had faith that there were good things to come.

> *Now that you have purified yourselves by obeying the truth so that you have sincere love for your brothers, love one another deeply, from the heart. For you have been born again, not of perishable seed, but of imperishable, through the living and enduring word of God.*
> *—1 Peter 1:22–23*

I had faith that God was my master healer, that He would mend my broken body. After all, faith is believing in what is not seen. The only images of a healthy me were in my mind. My outward appearance was that of a frail and weak person. Apart from being an infant, I had never before had to depend on so many people to take care of me. I had hit rock bottom.

To him who loves us and has freed us from our sins by his blood,
and has made us to be a kingdom and priests to serve his God and
Father—to him be glory and power for ever and ever! Amen.
—Revelation 1:5–6

Chapter 12

The weekend following my last chemotherapy treatment did not go according to my plans at all. Sunday evening, instead of Lyle going home (I was thankful he didn't), we went to the local emergency room. The whole night was somewhat of a fiasco from the start, but I am so thankful everything turned out all right in the end. I had developed horrendous chest pain. It was so bad that I actually thought I might be dying. Lyle wheeled me in to the waiting room, explaining to the front desk staff that I was a patient with cancer who was going through active treatments and that I was having chest pain and shortness of breath. I was very willing to wait my turn any time I went to be treated, but this, to me, was a medical emergency. I didn't even have a nurse come to check on me, or put me in a room separated from everyone else. After waiting for what seemed like hours, they did finally do a chest x-ray, but then they put me right back out in the waiting room.

Lyle was beside himself by this time. He felt things were not being taken care of as if it were a serious situation. I would have agreed with him if I had not been in so much pain. After a while, we were taken to a room and were greeted by a nurse and the physician's assistant. I proceeded to explain to them that I was undergoing radiation and chemo for vulvar cancer and that I was having chest pain accompanied by some shortness of breath. The physician's assistant asked me if I was having any other symptoms or any unusual bleeding. I did explain that I was having some bleeding in the areas currently being irradiated. I also informed her that my radiation oncologist was well aware of this. This information did not stop her from letting me know that she would have to do internal exams, to which my response was a firm, but polite, no. I already knew what was going on down there. I really wanted her to focus on why my chest felt as if it were being filled with cement.

He gives strength to the weary and increases the power of the weak.
—Isaiah 40:29

I was also pretty sure by that point that she did not know what vulvar cancer was. It is so important when you are going through treatment, for anything, that you are the advocate for your own health. Don't be afraid to speak up when you are seeking medical advice and treatment. You know your body better than anyone else, and you do have a voice when it comes to what is done with it.

It took some time, but the physician's assistant did send someone in to do lab work and to give me a GI cocktail (a Maalox–lidocaine mixture). That did seem to help my symptoms a little bit. They were now manageable enough to where I was no longer writhing in pain. I was exhausted but was now able to lie still. The last five weeks had caught up with me all at once. That was apparent with my lab results, which began to take a nosedive.

By the time the doctor finally came in, I was feeling better from the GI cocktail. He went over my risks, told me my labs were all right, and said that the likelihood of this being a blood clot was minimal, so he felt that a CT was not necessary. He asked me how I felt about that, and I said I was all right with it, because by that point, I no longer had any confidence in the care that was being provided to me. We opted to go home without the CT scan because the doctor didn't seem concerned. Of course, after we had been home for less than an hour, we were on our way back to the hospital. This time we were headed for Froedtert & the MCW. It just made sense to go there, since all of my treatments were being done there anyway. They would be able to access everything that I had done earlier through the electronic health records system.

Nothing was simple the second time around. Halfway to Froedtert & the MCW, Lyle had to pull over and call for an ambulance. A feeling of impending doom had washed over me, and I felt as if my chest was going to implode. It was as if my left lung was being turned to stone. The EMTs who arrived were very kind and professional. They worked together like a well-oiled machine. It reminded me of years past, when I worked for a brilliant private-practice doctor. He always said that excellent health care

He said to them, "Go into all the world and
preach the good news to all creation."
—Mark 16:15

should work like a bicycle chain, because if you are missing one link, it doesn't function properly.

These guys were definitely not missing a link. They immediately got me on a cardiac monitor and put me on an IV. My heart rate was up and I was shaking uncontrollably, but otherwise I was stable. Initially they were going to take me to the heart hospital, but since I was in no immediate cardiac danger, they granted my request to go to Froedtert & the MCW.

Upon my arrival there, the physician came in right away to examine me and go over my symptoms. While he was doing that, they hooked my IV line up and pushed some fluids, and then drew some more labs. They also gave me another GI cocktail, which again gave me some relief for a time. They insisted on a CT scan because they were concerned I might have an embolism. Those quick-read results came back negative, so I again opted to go home versus being admitted for observation. I know it sounds silly to opt to go home after visiting two emergency rooms in one night, but when you have been practically living at a hospital for over a month, it is the last place you want to be. After all, a blood clot was ruled out. I was just going to have to try to suck it up. They did send me home with a prescription for the GI cocktail, which we filled once we got back to town.

The pharmacy just added humor to the already crazy evening we were having. We got there at two in the morning, and even though there was not another soul in sight, we still had at least a twenty-minute wait to fill the prescription. We had become masters at waiting, so we pulled into the parking lot and talked for a bit. After the twenty minutes had passed, we went back around through the drive-through window. The pharmacist told us the prescription would not be covered by the insurance because Maalox was an over-the-counter medication. I was very excited to hear that it was available because I had not been able to find it anywhere. I immediately asked her if I could purchase it there. Then she told me it was no longer sold, but there were similar products available for purchase. Insurance companies. They always find the loopholes.

It didn't matter to me if it was covered or not. I needed the medication, so we politely asked her to fill the prescription anyway. Then we were on

It is God who arms me with strength and makes my way perfect.
—Psalm 18:32

our way. I felt bad for Lyle, because he still had almost an hour's drive home after he dropped me off. This left him with two hours to sleep before he had to go to work. Little did we know, we should have just opted to stay at the hospital.

I received a phone call early Monday morning from the nurse at the Cancer Center. They were calling me about my CT scan. My first thought was that they saw cancer in my lungs, but that was not the case. I was instructed to report back to the emergency department, because apparently, the quick read of my CT was just that, quick. They reviewed the scans that were read stat to ensure nothing was missed, and upon double checking the images they saw that I did actually have a pulmonary embolism. I was just relieved I did not have more cancer. I would gladly report back to the emergency department. At least I knew now that the pain was not something I was making up in my head. I called Lyle at work and told him the news. My son Roman drove me back to Froedtert & the MCW because it made no sense for Lyle to drive an hour to pick me up and then have to drive another hour to get me there, so Roman and I just met him at the hospital. He actually beat us there. His worried face was the first thing I saw when we pulled up.

They checked me in through the emergency room, and then I was transferred up to the floor for a few days' stay to monitor symptoms and get me going on blood thinners. It was actually a blessing in disguise. Yes, I said it: a blessing. I was able to finish out my last three days of radiation while I was there in the hospital. The wheelchair rides through the corridors were long, but not as long as being in a car for two hours a day. I was not upset that the clot had not been caught with the quick read. I was actually very impressed they had a double-check system in place and that the clot was caught. The staff handled it very professionally. The clot did buy me six months' worth of twice-a-day Lovenox injections, which make you feel like you are holding an angry bee up to your stomach for a few seconds when you are administering them, but you get used to them after a while. Another necessary evil, so to speak.

Humble yourselves, therefore, under God's mighty hand, that He may lift you up in due times.
—James 1:12

Social Media Post, April 26, 2016

Should be going home from Froedtert tomorrow after my last radiation treatment. Was admitted yesterday for a pulmonary embolism. Total fiasco Sunday. Starting to feel a little better. Thankful it was caught. Treatment done tomorrow, and still going as planned. Yahoo.

Wednesday finally came. I had completed my last radiation treatment. It was my turn to ring the bell when I left. From the day I'd started treatment, I'd looked forward to the time when it would be my turn to ring the bell. It was a celebration for everyone to hear that another one of us had made it through to the end of our treatments. It gave hope to those still going through treatments, a small reminder that their days were coming and to look to the future. The women in the radiation department also gave me a certificate of completion that was signed. I never stopped praying throughout this journey. Prayer is what kept me focused.

I was scheduled to see my radiation oncologist on Monday, along with one of her wound-care nurses, whom I enjoyed seeing. They were both wonderful. They always made sure I had enough supplies to care for my

I lift up my eyes to the hills—where does my help come from? My help comes from the Lord, the maker of heaven and earth.
—Psalm 121:1–2

wounds properly, and they were willing to spend as much time with me as I needed to ensure all of my questions were answered and my wounds were clean and dressed. My providers made me feel loved. They treated my cancer, but they also treated me like a human being. They talked with me and with my family, they held my hand, and they hugged me when I needed it. They listened more than they spoke. I think sometimes people in health care forget that those things are just as important as treating the disease. The providers I had would be great models for anyone to learn from. I was so thankful. I never felt as if I had to worry while I was there.

Social Media Post, April 28, 2016

Well, now I am ready to start healing. My lab work finally took a dump. My results look like poop, but I am determined to change that. For now, I don't really want to get up and do anything. Very sore. Just chilling in the recliner, praying for my skin to heal super quick. I go back to see the doctor on Monday to check in and see how things are progressing. I need to continue Lovenox shots twice a day for the next six months, but it beats getting new blood clots. Overall, I am doing good, by the grace of God. Without Him, I would be a hot mess right now. God bless you all.

Social Media Post, April 28, 2016

Please continue to share this. With new meds, unexpected hospital stays, and no income until the end of May now, it will be very tight. I know so many of you have helped so much, and I know that God will provide. You have all been such a blessing to me and my family. Please share this [GoFundMe page link] as much as you can and continue to pray. Thank you so much. God bless you.

One man gives freely, yet gains even more; another withholds unduly, but comes to poverty. A generous man will prosper; he who refreshes others will himself be refreshed.
—Proverbs 11:24–25

Chapter 13

A GoFundMe page was started by Lyle when I was diagnosed, and my best friend, Marcy, had thrown that amazing fund-raiser. The medical bills continued to pile up as procedures were done, and my insurance company was picky about what they would cover. My medications now cost me nothing to pick up, which was a huge blessing, but it was only because my out-of-pocket maximum had been met. I could choose to look at this as the cup being half full or half empty. I liked the idea of just being happy with the cup. My Lovenox alone would have cost hundreds of dollars a month if my insurer hadn't picked up the cost. Of course, that same insurance company decided that my radiation treatments were deemed "experimental" because I was receiving a higher dose of radiation to the areas with active cancer and lower doses to the surrounding tissue. According to them, I needed to belong to a trial group in order to have my radiation treatments approved, which I was not. That was my understanding of that whole mess anyways, and by that point, I was too sick and tired to care. It tacked on a substantial amount of money, but in the end, what was my life really worth? I couldn't sum it up in dollars. I tried to budget for the medical bills, but there seemed to be a new area I was paying for each step of the way. There were bills from the lab, pathology, radiology, the hospital, and the clinic, and then there were the specialists I was seeing to treat the side effects from the treatments. Most places will work with you, but some just want their bills paid now. They want you to beg, borrow, or steal to get them their money. Finances can weigh heavy on your soul if you let them, but God is good and He will provide. I spent a lot of my prayer time asking for my financial troubles to be ironed out. I remember being in a bind one month and short two hundred dollars for the rest of the bills. I had no clue where I was going to

Taste and see that the Lord is good; blessed is
the man who takes refuge in him.
—Psalm 34:8

get that money. My mother and my grandmother had already helped so much; I was not going to ask them for anything else.

I prayed, like always, for things to fall into place and for God to provide, just as He provides for the birds when they are in need. *"Look at the birds of the air; they do not sow or reap or store away in barns, and yet your heavenly Father leads them. Are you not much more valuable than they? Can any one of you by worrying add a single hour to your life?" Matthew 6: 26-27 NIV.* After all, a struggle is a struggle, whether it is physical, mental, or financial. We have all been there. That same day, I received a card from a family member I have never had the pleasure of meeting. She sent a little note in an envelope, which held a check for two hundred dollars. I cried. They were tears of joy, but I cried nonetheless. The financial burdens of being sick and trying to continue to hold things together are tremendous, and they go hand in hand with the emotional ups and downs of a hard diagnosis, a difficult treatment plan, and physical effects that wear you down. The devil always tried to ravage my spirit. Throughout this whole war I was waging, the enemy came at me from all sides relentlessly. I never ran short of miracles. That check was a miracle—just one of many that I experienced throughout this storm.

Social Media Post, May 3, 2016

It has been one week since my last radiation treatment. I now feel as if I have had a load of bricks dropped on my head. My white blood cell count is nonexistent, and if it does not come up by this Friday, then I will need a shot to give it a boost. I am also still anemic, but the CBC [complete blood count] is improving, so that is good. Skin is still a hot mess, but I do see improvements every day. Praise the Lord! This week has been rough, I am not going to lie. I am kind of a wet noodle (with a smile on my face). I can

Rejoice in the Lord always. I will say it again; Rejoice! The Lord is near. Do not be anxious about anything, but in everything, by prayer and petition, with thanksgiving, present your requests to God. And the peace of God, which transcends all understanding will guard your hearts and your minds in Christ Jesus.
—Philippians 4:4–7

hardly walk to the bathroom right now without falling on the floor, but this too will pass. Still seems strange that I am going through this, that I can't get up and do things, but it is the little things that sustain me, like enjoying my children and my grandchildren, breathing fresh air as it blows through an open window, listening to the birds chirp, and enjoying every moment that I am blessed with. There is always someone who is worse off. Pay it forward, even if it is only a smile or a kind gesture. Love you all! Have a great day!

My youngest daughter, Celese, helped me back and forth to the bathroom and did my wound care. I had resigned myself to the fact that I was still not afforded any dignity in this process. I am proud of her for being so strong and caring for me like it was no big deal at all. She and Kayla both just did what needed to be done, with no complaints and without making me feel any more uncomfortable than I already was. The rest of the kids were helpful in their own ways, such as taking the garbage out, cooking a meal, doing a load of laundry, or cleaning the house. They all stepped up and pitched in. Lyle continued to take care of what he could on the weekends when he was in town. I still felt as though my children were still looking to me for guidance through all of this, even though I was sick. I guess that once you are the head of the household, you are considered the heavy. It always made me think of my great-grandmother. Her name was Bertha, but everyone called her "Big Betty", which I always joked made her sound like a mob boss. My grandmother was "Little Betty," like Big Betty's number two. Big Betty ran her house with an iron fist, literally. She was the chief. The only person who really liked to argue with her and get a rise out of her was my great-grandfather. He would just laugh. It was fun to watch. There has been a long line of strong women in my family, strong and stubborn. You won't find one family member who would disagree with me on that one. I was no exception. I didn't want anyone hovering over me. I didn't want a fuss being made. I enjoyed the

One man gives freely, yet gains even more: another withholds unduly, but comes to poverty. A generous man will prosper; he who refreshes others will himself be refreshed.
—Proverbs 11:24–25

occasional visits for lunch, the cards to say "I am thinking of you," a dinner being made, and other acts of kindness, but overall, especially when all I wanted to do was lie there, I didn't want to be bothered. I had become a little frustrated that I had to rely on so many people to do very simple tasks, like walking, using the bathroom, making a sandwich, or even opening a bottle of water. God had all the right people placed in my life to help me do the things I could not. Even though I occasionally bucked the system, their presence was a gentle reminder that I was loved. It reminded me never to give up.

Social Media Post, May 6, 2016

Admitted to Froedtert & the MCW last night for fever. Feeling better today, but they might keep me one more night. Doc will let me know this afternoon. I am looking forward to starting to feel better ... one of these days. I have kind of fallen apart since my treatments have ended. But I am still smiling. Kids are a little freaked out, so keep 'em in your prayers. Love you all. Keep the faith.

Another hospitalization had my kids on edge. My labs tanked. Before I went to the hospital, my kids were having me check my temperature constantly. Every time someone would walk by me, they would feel my forehead. Following each temperature check was an urging to go to the hospital. I am pretty sure one of them called Lyle and told on me, because he came to town and took me in. I wanted to try to tough it out, even though I knew the protocol for patients with cancer was to go to the emergency room if a fever developed. I was just so tired. I wanted to sleep forever. I didn't want to move. The mere thought of moving was exhausting, but I put a smile on my face and allowed my family to shuffle me out to the truck for yet another adventure to the hospital.

I was admitted for observation and was allowed to go home the next day after my fever broke. Once my fever broke, I felt as if that was the

So then, those who suffer according to God's will, should commit themselves to their Faithful Creator and continue to do good.
—1 Peter 4:19

pivotal point for me. I had hit rock bottom, so I was going to be climbing upward from there. My goal was to get stronger. I made sure I was drinking enough water and eating better—even though food still tasted like nuts and bolts—taking my vitamins, and remaining positive. I had to continue to practice what I preached, with some days simply seeming a lot harder than others.

Chapter 14

When Mother's Day hit, I was extra emotional. I had been entertaining the thought of not being around for my children. I struggled with this thought the most on this day. I also thought about how my own mother would feel if I were suddenly gone. Throughout all of this, this day put a twist on how I had been looking at my disease. I hadn't ever really taken the time to think about how she felt, knowing that her baby was ill. I would have been beside myself if one of my children were going through this, so I could only imagine how helpless she felt. We also had almost two hours of distance between us, and she was already the caretaker for my grandmother, so she couldn't just pop in whenever she wanted to. I knew she wanted to be there, but I also knew that her circumstances made it very difficult. She did call me almost daily to check in, and she always made arrangements if she needed to be there to help with something. After all, who plans for their kid to have cancer? Who is mentally prepared for that? Even after everything I have been through personally, I would not be prepared.

Social Media Post, May 8, 2016

I want to wish a happy Mother's Day to all of you. How blessed you are to be that important part of your children's lives. Especially with this busy rat race we all seem to be stuck in, remember to love them with all of your heart, teach them so they will be able to make smart decisions for themselves, and be there for them to support them, even if you don't necessarily agree with what they are doing. God blessed you with your family. Honor Him by raising them up in His ways. Life is too short to wait for it to be a better time to make changes. Smile, laugh, and hug one another a lot. Never take

When Jesus spoke again to the people, he said, "I am the light of the world. Whoever follows me will never walk in darkness, but will have the light of life."
—John 8:12

each other for granted. Keep your promises, however silly they may seem. Happy Mother's Day, Sandra Hurtt and Betty Wellspring, two of the most amazing women whom I have had the pleasure to be raised by. I love you both so much. Happy Mother's Day to all of my amazing friends. I love you! Keep the faith!

Social Media Post, May 8, 2016, written by David Salas (my youngest son)

Happy Mother's Day to one of the greatest moms around! I know that life's been really tough for us lately, but even through it all you still stay strong for all of us. I wouldn't be the man I am today if it weren't for you. I am so grateful for the life you gave me. I hope you have a beautiful day, because you deserve it. I love you, Mama!

My children made my day. They spent Mother's Day hanging out with me, talking, and laughing. The best gift was given that I could ever ask for: their time. I really wasn't up for a anything physical, but the cards were great, and I just savored the time I got to spend with each and every one of them. Facing your own mortality makes you realize just how precious the time you spend with your loved ones is.

Finally, be strong in the Lord and in his mighty power.
—Ephesians 6:10

Chapter 15

Social Media Post, May 9, 2016

Happy Monday, everyone! So, back to the doctor tomorrow for updated labs and a game plan. Still healing. It has been a bit of a bumpy road, but I am doing a little better each and every day. Having a little difficulty with neuropathy in my feet and lower legs and in my fingers, but I am muddling through this one day at a time. God has truly blessed me. I am hoping the doctor will tell me I can start some type of physical therapy soon to build my stamina back up, because I swear I will never sit down for more than five minutes at a time once I am back to 100 percent. I think my recliner has a permanent butt imprint from me already, lol. I ask for continued prayers for all those fighting cancer, as I know each and every one of us knows someone with cancer or is in that position ourselves. If you want more people to pray, please list them—first name is fine—so we can add them to our individual prayer time. God bless you all.

My wound treatments were now being spaced out a little bit. I didn't have to go back for a week. This was great news, as I was in a lot of pain and the car rides were physically unpleasant. I did still look for and find reasons to enjoy them overall. I liked having someone to talk to. I spent many days at home entertaining myself, so the interaction was something I looked forward to.

My skin was raw, but it was mending. My new skin was rising from

> *No temptation has seized you except what is common to man.*
> *And God is faithful; he will not let you be tempted beyond*
> *what you can bear. But when you are tempted, he will also*
> *provide a way out so that you can stand up under it.*
> *—1 Corinthians 10:13*

the proverbial ashes. That is how I looked at it, anyway. It was as if I had been set on fire but was now being renewed. I can describe my spiritual growth throughout this journey in the same way, as can so many of the people who go through life-changing events.

Without God, I was cold and lost, but with God, the fire rose up within me and my mind. I was renewed as I was filled with the Holy Spirit. I know that to some, that may sound silly. I cannot express enough how God has changed my life. And no, I didn't pray and then things magically got better. If anything, they got harder. At every turn there seemed to be a new fight or a struggle, but I kept the faith. I learned to endure the trials without questioning God. My prayer life was filled; my soul, satisfied.

My greatest prayer continued to be answered, as I was given more time to continue to witness to my family and to as many others as possible. I prayed continually to God, asking that He use me as a living testimony of His grace and mercy, His healing, and His love for me and for all of us. I can honestly say that even if my prognosis were not what it had been, my prayers would not have changed, nor would my outlook on this journey. I can't say that the same would have been the case years ago. I was a believer, but my faith was weak. My walk with the Lord was clouded by my struggle to follow God's path and not my own.

Social Media Post, May 13, 2016

Happy Friday, everyone! On Monday I had an appointment. I don't have to go back for another week and a half now. It's nice not to have to drive to Froedtert & the MCW for a bit. No physical therapy yet; they want me to take it easy because of the pulmonary embolism. Blah, blah, blah. So I have accomplished my first task of walking up and down the block—I know, sounds super exciting, doesn't it? I still get winded pretty easily, so it is a pretty amazing accomplishment. Will have to do the Lovenox shots for the next five and a half months. My stomach is starting to look like a black-and-blue pincushion, but I would rather deal with that than have

I pray that you may be active in sharing your faith, so that you will have a full understanding of every good thing we have in Christ.
—Philemon 1:6

more clot complications. I have another PET scan July 28, with an appointment the first week in August. They will tell me then if they got all the cancer or not, so the waiting game begins. Cancer affects everyone, folks. Our mothers, our fathers, our brothers, our sisters, our children, ourselves. Everyone knows someone, and it seems like every time we turn around, someone else is affected. Please pray for those in the battle, and for their families. We don't always get the answers we want, but with God, all things are possible. We all have our struggles, but we also are truly blessed. My prayer is that you see the blessings you have today. Keep the faith. I love you all.

By this point, even though the actual treatments were completed, I had become more and more frustrated with the progression of my overall health. I was probably my toughest critic. Just walking up a flight of stairs made me feel as if I had an elephant on my back. It was difficult for me to walk one city block without gasping for air, and I still felt as if I needed to take a nap in between doing things like washing the dishes, sweeping the floor, or making the bed. These were all things that I used to do in a flash. My coworkers would have been amazed by how slow I was moving, especially since *slow* was never in my vocabulary before this. My struggle had morphed into an emotional one.

My physical difficulties were now weighing heavy on my state of mind. I had to pray for patience. Oddly enough, my prayers were answered with instances where I needed to practice patience—*practice* being the key word. But I kept praying for patience, and God kept presenting me with scenarios so I could practice, practice, practice. It took me a while to understand that I was getting exactly what I'd asked for, so I changed what I was praying for and thanked God for allowing me to exercise my ability to use patience even when I didn't want to.

My healing had plateaued; I was no longer making any great strides in improvement. I was stuck, in a physical rut, but I was still smiling, although I joked that I was smiling now only because I had lost my mind.

I have been crucified with Christ and I no longer live, but Christ lives in me. The life I live in the body, I live by faith in the Son of God, who loved me and gave himself for me.
—Galatians 2:20

That wasn't true. I was actually smiling because I continued to find ways to count my blessings throughout my days. Things I had not stopped to notice before amid my very busy, fast-paced life came screeching to a halt. I have said it before, and I will say it again: I don't ever doubt for one moment that God has a great sense of humor. I am convinced He most certainly does.

Social Media Post, May 14, 2016

Okay, I can only laugh. So I am stuck, you know, resting—and my television dies. I don't know whether I am just laughing at the circumstances or if I am laughing because that was the last straw … lol! Keeping the faith!

Resting seemed to be the one thing that I had gotten remarkably good at. I have excelled at binge-watching television series from Netflix and Pureflix. I also filled my time with reading books, studying my Bible, coloring, cross-stitching, and even dabbling with writing, but most of the time I sat alone watching television. Family and friends have their own lives to deal with, so the television had become a comforting friend, filling the atmosphere with other voices besides my own.

When my television died, I wished I was able to bring it back to life somehow. What I did do was to try to troubleshoot the problem. Remember that patience I talked about earlier? I know, you already get the joke. I got another chance to practice it. I did get a pleasant gentleman on the computer through live chat, who walked me through the troubleshooting tips until we realized that I would need to have the TV repaired. Repairs would basically cost as much as a new television, which explains why the television repairman has gone extinct. I thanked the gentleman for his assistance and began researching an inexpensive replacement for my deceased counterpart.

I am not saying this because I am in need, for I have
learned to be content whatever the circumstances.
—Philippians 4:11

Social Media Post, May 14, 2016

Okay, lol, my showerhead just broke off now. Lol. Who has seen this movie? Can you name it? Yeah, I am still smiling. ... Keep the faith.

The same day I buried my television, my showerhead broke off, while I was standing in there getting ready to take a nice, warm, relaxing shower, to destress from my rather long and pointless conversation trying to fix my television. I actually laughed out loud when it came off in my hands. Couldn't help myself. What else was I going to do? I eventually got my showerhead fixed and managed to find an inexpensive off-brand to replace my broken television. Everything was right in my world again. I certainly could have lived without a replacement television in the living room, especially since I had a television in my bedroom. I could have just as easily lay in there when I wanted to watch something, but I enjoyed the occasional sighting of a teenager from my recliner in the living room. Part of me struggled with the decision to replace the television because I felt as if I was being greedy, but watching a movie with my family, or losing myself in a show, allowed me to escape my reality for a spell, which was a godsend, since I was pretty run down.

I couldn't let guilt take control. The devil was just looking for ways to put his two cents in anywhere he could. It is all right to want things for yourself. It is all right to pray for things for yourself and your family. Just don't lose sight of what is important. God is not going to give you anything He doesn't want you to have. The old bumper sticker reading "He who dies with the most toys wins" is wrong on so many levels, but nothing says you can't pray, ask for, and receive the blessings God has in store for you.

Test me O Lord and try me, examine my heart and my mind; for
your love is ever before me, and I walk continually in your truth.
—Psalm 26:2–3

Chapter 16

I was scheduled to go back and see my radiation oncologist on Tuesday of the following week. I had been taking my vitamins every day and watching what I was eating, hoping that it would make a positive change in my lab results. My daughter Kayla was leaving that day as well. It was a sad day. I have missed her dearly since she left to go back home. She always told me, when she was a little girl, that she was going to live with me forever and ever. She was the first to move what feels like a million miles away. I can't wait until the day she decides to move back to Wisconsin.

Social Media Post, May 20, 2016

Happy Friday, everyone! Back to the doctor on Tuesday for labs and a visit. Hopefully WBC [white blood cell] count and H/H [hemoglobin and hematocrit] will be much improved. Having a few other complications at this time, but hoping my worries about those will be put to rest by the doc on Tuesday. My daughter Kayla Arneson is leaving Tuesday. My heart is heavy, as not only have I been blessed by all of her help over the past few weeks, but also I have truly enjoyed her being here. Please pray for her safe travel home and for better news form the doc on Tuesday. I am also asking for prayers for strength, both physical and emotional. This has been a really difficult few months, probably the hardest of my life and my family's. Treatments have finished, and my body kind of feels apart, I feel as if I have a little as well. It is like I have been holding my breath forever, and now that I can breathe, I forgot hew. So please continue to pray. I know I keep asking, but without God, I would have been more of a hot mess than I feel I am already. God has been so good to me, continually blessing me

> ***Dear friends, if our hearts do not condemn us, we have confidence before God and receive from him anything we ask, because we obey his commands and do what pleases him.***
> ***—1 John 3:21–22***

through this storm. I don't want to lose sight of that. I love you all and miss you! Happy Friday! Have a great weekend. It is supposed to be beautiful outside.

I did go see my radiation oncologist, but not on Tuesday. I didn't want to be gone when Kayla left. I wanted to spend as much time with her as I could before she had to leave for the airport. I rescheduled my doctor's appointment for later in the week. When that time came, I discussed some pain that I had been having in my hip and groin. The pain was on the same side that my cancer had been on. My doctor ordered an MRI, looking for the source of my pain and symptoms, with one of those possibilities being more cancer. I have come to the conclusion that anytime I have an ache or a pain, I am going to think I have cancer again. I am not sure why I should have cancer, because honestly, there was no pain until a week or so before my original diagnosis, but it is always the first thing that pops into my head. If I have a headache, it's brain cancer. If I have heartburn, it must be esophageal cancer. If I have middle-back pain, it must be kidney cancer. If I have urinary issues, it must be bladder cancer. The list goes on and on. I have discussed this with other survivors, who all have similar thoughts. I have been told that this way of thinking may get a little better with time but usually doesn't go away. The truth is, cancer doesn't scare me as much anymore since we have already had a pretty good fight. There is always going to be a winner and a loser in that battle. I am fortunate enough to be a winner thus far. I am not ready to go anywhere yet, but it has been made painfully aware to me that it is about God's plan, not mine.

Social Media Post, June 16, 2016

Had two MRIs done recently, for newly developed symptoms … looking for more cancer. … Praise the Lord! No cancer seen! I need to see a neurologist now, but I will take that over cancer. God is good. I was, honestly, nervous, but my faith kept me strong. I can do all things through Christ who strengthens me. If you are dealing

This is the message we have heard from him and declare to you: God is light; in him there is no darkness at all.
—*1 John 1:5*

with struggles, turn your eyes to the sky. His love and mercies are real. Please keep praying. My symptoms are still bothersome. I tire quickly, which still drives me crazy, and now I'm dealing with neuropathy that goes up to my thighs. But through it all, I am thankful and blessed. Love you, my friends. Keep the faith.

With the increase in side effects from my previous chemotherapy treatments, some days, some days involved more nothing than something, while others actually allowed me to complete a task without taking a nap. I never lacked for things to do; because of my antsy nature, I always managed to find something to occupy my time. My body was doing its own thing. It seemed to be on strike. It had a mind of its own and didn't want to cooperate with any efforts I made to get back to healthy state. It took me a while to admit that maybe I was just not listening to what my body was trying to tell me. I am sure I set my expectations too high and tried to push myself too hard. I wanted my old self back. I was the caretaker, the head of my household and of my family: the boss. The step I needed to take to give total and complete control to God was huge for me. I wasn't just handing over control in the throes of an illness but in my everyday life, whether things improved or not. I had given Him control of my physical health. I trusted Him and I had faith, but I was still trying to maintain some semblance of authority over the rest of my life. My mind needed to be on board 100 percent. My idea of how things should go in my life was weighing heavily on my emotions and affecting my outlook on things. I built up situations and people only to be saddened. Once I realized what my struggle really was, those situations became less of a disappointment to me. I seemed to be fighting myself, my expectations of how I thought things should be. I knew I couldn't heal in my own time; it was God's timing, God's plan. I knew people were not going to do things as I had planned out in my head just because I thought it was what they should be doing. I had to listen and be willing to follow God's lead in all aspects of my life, not just in the areas I picked. I had to be content with where I was in my treatment plan and not continually *want* to be how I was, because I was not there yet and might not ever be. I had to

In my distress, I cried to the Lord, and He answered me.
—Psalm 120:1

be content with the me that was healing, the broken me, and allow God to take control of it all, so He could build me up. I had to stop expecting others to do as I thought they should be and learn to be content with what they did do. I needed to be completely in tune with God. I needed to have peace within myself.

Social Media Post, June 27, 2016

Happy Monday, my friends. I have not updated my status for a little bit, so here is the short and skinny, lol. I am still struggling with fatigue and shortness of breath. (The humidity definitely does not help.) I am still restricted to walking, and driving is difficult and not encouraged by physicians since I have neuropathy in both legs and really have to watch my foot placement, even when going up and down stairs, which I don't do often because of the shortness of breath. My brain is going stir-crazy because my body is still not cooperating well, but I'm not complaining, because I am finding things to stay busy, in between naps of course, lol. I am making tamales, which is very time-consuming, but with help from my daughters, it is manageable. And I am able to rest when I need to. I have also completed numerous large cross-stitch projects (Christmas presents for some). It has been nice to be able to spend the time with my children, even though I miss working. I know I am nowhere near ready to go back. I will be glad when I can start exercising more, because my stamina sucks, but I have faith that it will get better in time as well. I have had plenty of time to cultivate my relationship with God throughout my time off and through this journey. I am thankful for that. I am keeping the faith and still fighting the good fight. I am thankful God has given me such an awesome support structure, Lyle Torres, Ryann Arneson, Brianna Rex, Roman Arneson, David Salas, Celese Salas, Grace Salas, Kayla Arneson, Triston Torres, Marcy Prochnow, Sandra Hurtt, Andrew Bodnar, Betty Wellspring, and Sheryl Hanson.

Dear friends, I urge you, as aliens and strangers in the world,
to abstain from sinful desires, which war against your soul.
—1 Peter 2:11

Everyone continued to be so helpful as I dealt with the side effects from chemo. I began driving less and less as the neuropathy began to take more of a toll on me. I was having a hard time feeling how much pressure I was putting on the gas pedal, and sometimes I had to look, because I could not feel the brake pedal when I would transfer my foot over to it.

Driving became scary. I no longer felt safe driving a car for anything longer than a quick run to the store a couple of blocks away. This further limited my ability to leave the house, because I was still not capable of walking very long distances. Now any time I went anywhere, I had a small posse tagging along to make sure I didn't fall apart. My kids watched me like a hawk. They tag-teamed to ensure I wasn't attempting to do anything I wasn't supposed to. I still couldn't lift anything heavier than a gallon of milk, so carrying laundry or picking up my grandchildren was out of the question. My grandson's weight at the time was the same as three gallons of milk, so lifting him was a definite no-no. My granddaughter, Lily, understood and would just take my hand and tell me everything was going to be all right. She knew her geema couldn't pick her up because she still wasn't well. She never stopped telling me everything was all good, though. To this day, every time she sees me, she moves my shirt and checks for my port site, and then she hugs me and tells me it's okay. It is almost like she figures that if it is still there, then I am still sick. But her messages to me are always positive and full of love.

His divine power has given us everything we need for life and godliness through our knowledge of him who called us by his own glory and goodness.
—2 Peter 1:3

Geema and Lily being silly.

As the days grew long and the nights grew longer, I became increasingly aware that the symptoms in my legs, and the lightheadedness, were actually getting worse. My POTS (postural orthostatic tachycardia syndrome) had progressed to the point where just changing positions, bending down, or even singing while standing in church made me see stars and want to black out. The tingling in my legs increased as well. Now there was an added transient stinging sensation, almost like little electric shocks that would zap me up and down my legs. My knees were also giving out on me daily. Stairs were my new nemesis. But I was thankful there was carpeting on my front hall steps now, because it padded my landing on a few occasions. The basement stairs hadn't been so friendly.

Social Media Post, July 1, 2016

Amen! Peace, love, and mercy is found in the storm if you trust God! If you don't, you are truly thrown back and forth like a ship in a raging storm.

Give me understanding, and I will keep your law and obey it with all my heart. Direct me in the path of your commands for there I find delight.
—Psalm 119:34–35

My prayer list continued to grow, with people I knew, or people they knew, who were struggling with cancer, struggling with life. My coworkers, friends, old neighbors—the list was long. Everyone knows someone fighting cancer. According to the World Health Organization, worldwide cases of cancer are predicted to increase by over four and a half 40 million. (Hume and Christensen 2014). That is a lot of people. My cancer was rare. Many women I have talked to had no clue 41) what vulvar cancer was, or even what a vulva was for that matter. Even though vulvar cancer is not as prevalent as breast cancer, the information should still be made known.

I was surprised every time I had to give a small anatomy lesson to explain my cancer. There were even some clinical professionals who didn't know what vulvar cancer is, so how are the rest of us supposed to be informed when they don't even give it a thought? That is why I wanted to bring this cancer into the limelight. Women need to be educated. Early detection for any cancer is important. I got lucky, because I ignored the signs. I thought they would just go away. It wasn't until I had pain in my groin that I started to complain. The reason my groin hurt was because the cancer had already invaded my lymph nodes. I want women to be informed and to know their bodies well enough not to ignore changes, and to pursue answers when they experience such changes. If your physician doesn't give you answers that bring you peace of mind, you get a second opinion. After all, it is your life.

Social Media Post, July 7, 2016

My prayer is for everyone, especially my friends Julie Benner, Steve Koss, Phyllis Orth, and Deb (and me), and all those around the world. Cancer sucks, but it also changed my life in some amazing ways.

Be strong and courageous. Do not fear or be in dread of them, for it is the Lord your God who goes with you. He will not leave you or forsake you.
—Deuteronomy 31:6

Chapter 17

New goal: I was determined to get to my mother's house for the Fourth of July and celebrate the holiday with my family. This was important to me because now, more than ever, I wanted to spend as much time as I could with the people I loved most in this world. Memories are not created staring at the TV or your smartphone, but by enjoying the people around you, wherever you are. My oldest son, Roman, was unable to come with us because of his work schedule, and my three youngest children were with their father, but everyone else was able to attend. Brianna and our two grandchildren rode with us. Ryann and Triston drove separately and met us in Janesville.

My mother has always been a great party planner. We spent the day swimming, playing games, eating, and enjoying one another's company. In the evening, we all watched as Ryann and Trit gave us an amazing backyard fireworks show. The little ones clapped and went from lap to lap, watching in awe. I think the adults spent more time watching the children's reactions to the fireworks. After spending a few hours around the fire, laughing and overindulging in s'mores, we all retired for the evening. The next day, we headed to my brother's house to enjoy the Janesville parade. It was amazing. It was so different from the parades I was used to seeing. The kids lined the streets with their bags, awaiting the handfuls of candy being thrown. It was a family-friendly small-town atmosphere. It was a great feeling to be able to relax and enjoy this with my kids and grandkids. Unfortunately, it was also short-lived.

Halfway through the parade, we received a phone call from my ex-husband. Our oldest son, Roman, was in the hospital being evaluated for a possible stroke. Nothing had prepared me for that phone call. I

Remind the people to be subject to rulers and authorities, to be obedient, to be ready to do whatever is good, to slander no one, to be peaceable and considerate, and to show true humility toward all men.
—Titus 3:1–2

immediately wanted to take this problem from Roman, to make him better, to be back in my hometown in an instant, but we had a ninety-minute ride home. It was the longest car ride I have ever taken. We prayed all the way home.

We went directly to the hospital. Roman was still in the emergency department, waiting for a room to open up. They were admitting him for observation. His blood pressure was still coming down. Thankfully, a stroke was ruled out. There were still health concerns, but these were things he could work on and improve over time. Praise the Lord.

Being in the hospital on the Fourth of July was depressing for Roman. He wanted to be with his family. He always loved fireworks, even as a baby. I took him when he was three and a half months old, and he just stared up at the sky in awe and wonder. Some of his brothers and sisters knew he would miss that, so they each took a firework and ran up to the hospital, which was only a few blocks from our house. When they were all in position, they called up to Roman's room and told him to look out his window. Once they saw him, they simultaneously lit their fireworks, and then they ran. Since their brother couldn't join them in celebrating, they brought a little piece of the celebration to him.

Social Media Post, July 7, 2016

Happy Thursday, everyone! I hope everyone had a great Fourth of July. I enjoyed being able to visit with family. Even though one of my children had a health scare on the Fourth, everyone is doing well. Please pray for my family. I would go into detail, but it is not my info to put out there. It's scary when something happens to one of your children though. I had a fleeting moment where I questioned God. Like, why? What have I done that deserves one trial after another? But then I realized what I was doing, and put my trust and faith in Him, knowing that he has a plan and a purpose for everything that we experience. As much as cancer sucks, it has made positive changes in my life as well. It has restored a broken faith, and filled me with the blessings and joy of

Praise be to the Lord, to God our Savior, who daily bears our burdens.
—Psalm 68:19

the Lord. That is my prayer for my children and my friends—for everyone, really. I am still very fatigued, and I fight with myself daily to move more than I want to. I can now breathe a little easier since my son Ryann Arneson showed up with the gift of an air conditioner so his mama wouldn't be huffing and puffing in the humid heat. Love you. I still huff and puff a bit, but I am cool doing it now, lol. I would encourage everyone to do something kind for someone today and every day, maybe without them even knowing you did it. Be a blessing to others. You will see how much joy it actually brings to you. I love you all. Please continue to pray for all those struggling with something in their lives. We all have our individual trials. Keep the faith.

Chapter 18

Good morning, everyone! Happy Tuesday. (Not so happy? Right now, think of three things you can be grateful for today, so get happy!) I haven't posted an update in a while, so I figured I better fill in the blanks. I have my PET scan (first one since treatments) on July 28. I am a little nervous, but it is in God's hands. Whatever the outcome is, I will get through it one day at a time. I do see the neurologist at Froedtert & the MCW next week. I think they are looking at the possibility of a definitive MS diagnosis, because of the new symptoms that have popped up since my treatments. I am still nursing my pulmonary embolism. Three more months of twice daily pesky little blood-thinning shots, and more fatigue and shortness of breath than I care to deal with, but I think (and again, for those of you who know me, you will laugh) God is trying to teach me to slow down and have patience. Can I get an amen there? Lol! I am still struggling with this one. My brain wants to go, go, go, but my body wants to lie there. Talk about war of the worlds, body vs. brain. Brain is losing, lol. I will be glad when I can start doing more than walking and will be happy when I can walk a flight of stairs without feeling like my lungs are going to implode, but at least I can make it up the stairs. I miss everyone! God bless all of you; keep the faith! Things might seem rough, but the blessings we overlook daily are the real joyful moments we are missing. My prayer is you will see those blessings.

The side effects from chemo were relentless. They continued to steadily creep into my life. It was a constant fight to focus on the future, when all my body wanted to do was take a stroll down memory lane. My legs were heavy, and the pins-and-needles feeling was overwhelming at times. I also had tunnel vision, accompanied by the feeling of an impending blackout, balance issues, and generalized weakness.

My gait was proof of my balance; I walked like I'd just left the tavern. The stairs were something I had to ascend and descend carefully, and any movement quicker than a snail's pace caused a nauseous, dizzy feeling. Even the motion of cars moving around me when I drove made me want to vomit, and caused a dizziness that made my arms and legs feel like rubber. Every day was a fight to conduct myself like everything was all right on the outside, even though the battle was still raging on the inside.

Social Media Post, July 20, 2016

I just want to say thank you so much to all of my friends and family for your support and prayers. You all mean so much to me. I am truly blessed to have you all in my life in one way or another. God has blessed me. So, spread the love and keep the faith. I get your cards and encouragements at just the right time, always. God's timing is perfect. You never know how much those little kind acts like a card in the mail, or a phone call, a message, or a drop-in for lunch really mean to someone until you are on the receiving end. Thank you, thank you, thank you. I love you guys!

Healing from anything in life is not something that fits into a cookie-cutter mold. One person could heal within four weeks, while another may take four months—and for others it may take a year or even longer. Complications arise; circumstances differ. The only thing that doctors can do is give an estimated time frame and hope for the best.

I love to be involved in caring for others, and I miss working. My cardiologist told me that the lightheaded feelings I got were probably due to the POTS and the fact that I was so deconditioned. The pulmonary embolism hadn't helped my cause; it only exacerbated my existing conditions. In order for me to feel better, I was going to need to build up my physical endurance and work on my cardiac fitness. This became especially frustrating for me, because in order to do that, I had to be able to work out, but I was still only medically cleared to walk.

For God gave us a spirit not of fear but of power and love and self-control.
—2 Timothy 1:7

Social Media Post, July 27, 2016

I am trying really hard to stay positive. God wants me on a different path … clearly. I just got off the phone with my employer. Since I have been out for six months (due to cancer—major surgery—followed by chemo and radiation) and am not cleared or ready to go back yet, I will be terminated. I have watched this happen to so many people before me who have had to deal with major illness, and it definitely adds to the stress, although I am trying very hard not to worry about this. I am not up to par yet. I saw a neurologist yesterday who ordered more tests because of my symptoms. I want to work. I love my patients and coworkers, but I am trying to do what I need to in order to heal properly. I have a pulmonary embolism. I get short of breath, dizzy, and very fatigued. I would like nothing better than to be able to run around like I used to. Those of you who have worked with me know how I work. Lazy, slow, and sloppy is not part of my work ethic. I am ranting. I am sorry. Been there almost ten years; feeling so frustrated right now. Please pray for this situation.

Social Media Post, August 1, 2016

PET scan results tomorrow …

It was a very long weekend awaiting the PET scan results. There was a lot of praying and positive thinking going on in my house. There are a lot of things that go through your head when you are awaiting news that you know will have a profound impact on how your life is played out. You wonder if everything you have endured for the past months was enough to fight the cancer that was growing inside of you, or if you will have to move on to more extensive treatment options. I tried not to give it too much thought, because I knew that if I did, I would be consumed by it. I knew, in reality, I would just have to deal with the results, because worrying about what they were was not going to change them.

As for you, brothers, do not grow weary in doing good.
—2 Thessalonians 3:13

Social Media Post, August 2, 2016

To God be the glory! MY PET scan today shows I am cancer-free! Amen! Hallelujah! Hopefully I will be able to start physical therapy soon. I need to do this not only to build strength up, but also to deal with lymphedema in my right leg. Next hurdle, pulmonary embolism. With three short months of Lovenox shots left, I am well on my way to recovery. Each day I strive to be stronger than the next. It has been a struggle, but I am determined to get back on my feet and be better than ever. I know God has a plan for me. I am so thankful and blessed.

The outcome of my PET scan was nothing short of a miracle. God placed the right people in my path. My family and friends supported me at every turn. My care providers who took my case as a challenge told me that they were fighting for my cure. Six months ago, I could have been given palliative care, and now I had been told I was cancer-free. I could live with the side effects for however long it took to get rid of them, if I got rid of them. I was alive and cancer-free. I knew I would never take my health for granted again. O the time I had wasted in my past, trying to impress people, getting so caught up in the world, our busy, fast-paced world that seemed to mow right over me in my time of need. It didn't stop. The show still had to go on. I found out quickly how replaceable I was in areas of my life that I had lifted up as so important. When I look back on that now, I know my relationship with God is first and foremost, as He never left my side through my ordeal. He made me who I was, who I am today. I am irreplaceable to my family and friends. That is the part of my life that I always took for granted. I missed out on so much, time that I can't get back. But my eyes are wide open now. I am on fire for the Lord, and I hold my family dear. God has given me a miraculous story to share.

For to set the mind on the flesh is death, but to set the mind on the Spirit is life and peace.
—Romans 8:6

Social Media Post, August 17, 2016

Amen. I am living proof of this. Stage 4 cancer with metastasis six months ago, and as of now, I am cancer-free. That is a miracle. God is good all the time. I felt His presence daily, especially when I was at my lowest points. I seek Him first in all things. My life is filled with blessings. Keep the faith.

Even though I had not yet been released to go back to work, I had a clean bill of health from a cancer standpoint. I was ready to begin some type of therapy. My cardiologist gave the okay for me to get registered with the Livestrong program at our local YMCA in September. I looked forward to that. I knew it would be only a matter of time before I received that dreaded phone call from the human resources department, because the long-term disability company had contacted me the day of my appointment to get my status before I'd even had a chance to go to my doctor's appointment. I think that dealing with them was just as exhausting as dealing with the cancer itself.

Social Media Post, August 19, 2016

HR at my job is quick. My date of separation/termination is August 18, 2016. Same day as my doctor appointment. I want to tell all of my work family how much I value your friendship. I have truly loved working with all of you. There is a new door opening for me. I want to complete my master's degree, so I am trying not to be sad about this. I knew it was coming. Just kind of surreal to actually hear the words. I am so blessed though, with the love of God; my family; my love, Lyle Torres; and all my friends. This has been an emotional six months, for all of us, as I battled with my cancer, diagnosis, and treatments, but a fresh page in my life is turning, and I am keeping the faith. God has a plan. Love you all. God bless you.

The loss of my job added to my already overloaded emotional state. I think I was more frustrated by the fact that I had given a great deal of

Arise, for it is your task, and we are with you; be strong and do it.
—Ezra 10:4

myself to my work at the expense of my family. Until now, I hadn't seen it that way. I had been a dedicated employee who was there for her coworkers and her patients. I picked up extra shifts to be helpful. I soaked up whatever could be taught so that I could be beneficial to the organization. I strived to do my best, and many nights I came home too exhausted to do anything else. I knew that in the end, it came down to making a business decision. It was not personal. It felt that way though. I was told I could reapply for a position in the next six months and not lose my seniority. I would still have to work my way up the ladder as far as my pay rate went. I had pushed and worked really hard to get to where I was at the time; I didn't think I could do that again. Actually, I didn't think I *wanted* to do that again. I was not going to put my family behind my work again. This was the hard life lesson, that no matter how hard I work, I am replaceable at work. My family had always been more important to me than my work; I just couldn't see it before. I took them for granted, figuring that they would always just be there. One of my daughters lives states away now, and I worked crazy hours most of her teenage years, when she lived with me. What I missed, I can never get back. That was my true sadness at the time of my dismissal.

Social Media Post, September 1, 2016

You can believe in God now or later. Now is better. It took events during my cancer treatments to really open my eyes to the truth. My prayer for everyone is that it doesn't take a life-altering event for you to see as well. God loves you. Keep the faith.

Tragedy strikes everyone's life. My prayers are filled with requests that people see the truth before they experience the storms. I am okay with being called a Jesus freak. *Christianity* has become a dirty word that people whisper. Christians continue to be persecuted all over the world, just for

Praise the Lord, my soul, and forget not all his benefits—who forgives all your sins and heals all your diseases, who redeems your life from the pit and crowns you with love and compassion, who satisfies your desires with good things so that your youth is renewed like the eagle's.
—Psalm 103:2–5

their beliefs. I will shout it from the rooftops, but I find it sad that with all of the freedoms we have in this country, the one that seems to be most offensive to people is being a Christian. My faith in Christ brought me strength when I was at my weakest. It brought me comfort when I was anxious and afraid. It brought me love when I was alone, and it brought me peace when I felt as if I could never feel peace again. Where do you find your comfort, your hope, and your strength? Do you look to the Lord in those times but forget Him the moment things start going well? I have found a great peace in my life through this journey. I pray you find peace as well. That is why I wanted to share my story, my incredible miraculous story. I want to listen. I want to weep with you, laugh with you, and rejoice and celebrate with you. I want you to celebrate with me, because I made it to my forty-seventh birthday, and with the way the year started, I wasn't sure I was going to.

The Lord is near to all who call on him, to all who call on him in truth. He fulfills the desires of those who fear him; he hears their cry and saves them.
—Psalm 145:18–19

Social Media Post, September 2, 2016

I want to say I am thankful for my mother, Sandra Hurtt, on this day, and every day ... but this day, forty-seven years ago, you chose to bring me into this world, giving up a part of yourself to be a mother. Thank you so much, Mom. I couldn't have asked for a better one. I love you.

It had been a busy couple of weeks. I got married on August 20. It was raining, of course. But our children came together and made it a beautiful day for us. They all worked so hard, transforming Roman and Brianna's backyard into a wedding wonderland. Our service was short but filled with love. I felt as if I was floating on cloud nine that day. Actually, most days I felt that way when I was with Lyle.

Through our conversations in past years, we discovered that we had been in the same place for most of our lives, but it wasn't until seven years ago that we actually met. God's timing is perfect. We were both in the right place at the right time, when He wanted us to be.

Our first dance as husband and wife was in the rain, and it was as if the heavens were pouring down on us. It was so romantic. Who needs sunshine when you can have a warm summer's rain falling down while "Healing Rain" is being played in the background? (Thank you, Miss Sheryl.) My granddaughter called me Princess Geema, and for the day, I was no longer struggling with anything. I was a princess. We were surrounded by our family, and the Lord's blessings were upon us.

Be completely humble and gentle; be patient, bearing with one another in love.
—Ephesians 4:2

Social Media Post, September 3, 2016

My husband always finds the most beautiful roses. I want to say thank you to everyone for the birthday wishes, and for all of your support and love through my journey with cancer. The year 2016 has been an emotional one, but my life and faith will be forever changed for the better because of it. When death is right there, and you are so exhausted from putting up a good fight, you are reminded what is important, and many times it was things I allowed myself to be too busy for before—more time with the kids, grandkids, family, prayer, serving others, smiling, and sometimes just taking in a beautiful sunrise. Thank you. God bless you all. Keep the faith.

But he said to me, "My grace is sufficient for you, for my power is made perfect in weakness." Therefore, I will boast all the more gladly about my weaknesses, so that Christ's power may rest on me. That is why, for Christ's sake, I delight in weaknesses, in insults, in hardships, in persecutions, in difficulties. For when I am weak, then I am strong.
—2 Corinthians 12:9–10

Our first dance as husband and wife.

Love is patient, love is kind. It does not envy, it does not boast, it is not proud. It does not dishonor others, it is not self-seeking, it is not easily angered, it keeps no record of wrongs. Love does not delight in evil but rejoices with the truth. It always protects, always trusts, always hopes, always perseveres. Love never fails. But where there are prophecies, they will cease; where there are tongues, they will be stilled; where there is knowledge, it will pass away.
—1 Corinthians 13:4–8

Chapter 19

Shortly after I lost my job, I received a letter in the mail detailing the insurance coverage being extended to me and my children through COBRA, if I chose to keep my former employer's health-care coverage. The letter clearly outlined the costs for the next four months for the four of us. It added up to over four thousand dollars to keep that insurance. Wow. I knew I couldn't do that even if I wanted to. My disability barely covered my outgoing payments and my groceries. I certainly couldn't add a bill that would be over a thousand dollars a month. I wondered how anyone could actually afford this. What a predicament it must put people in. I know that is how I felt.

Social Media Post, September 8, 2016

Joke of the day: COBRA insurance coverage. Enough said.

I didn't worry about it. I couldn't worry about it, because, again, worry never changed anything. It just stole my joy from the present moment. Besides, I had a party to plan. That was much more exciting than fretting over insurance. Lyle and I had decided that since we'd had a small wedding, we wanted to share our celebration with our extended family and friends, so we reserved a location at a local park and sent out invitations. So many people volunteered to help with food by bringing a dish to pass. That was such a tremendous help, since we were doing the cooking ourselves. There was a pavilion on the site we rented, but it was a structure without sides, and I was a little worried about the weather. I didn't want my grandmother to be uncomfortable or cold. I really wanted her to enjoy spending time with family she didn't get to see very often anymore.

Social Media Post, September 9, 2016

I am praying for good weather tomorrow, but I am determined to have a good time even if it rains, lol.

It rained. I have to admit, I did freak out a little bit in the morning because the wind was blowing so hard. I thought, *Oh God, please let this day be a good one.* I had lost sight of the fact that it was already a good day. It was a day that the Lord had made, and rain was on the menu that day— not my menu, but God's menu—and I was to be glad in it. We did manage to get some tent side panels up on one of the walls to protect the pavilion from the wind a little bit. The panels actually held up fairly well. In the end, it was a beautiful day. The winds died down, the sun came out, and it warmed up. It was as if God pushed away the clouds with His mighty hands and He smiled down on us, enveloping us with the warm rays of the sun. Friends and family came, the kids played, and I had worried about the weather for nothing. It ended up being an unforgettable day. At the end of it, we were exhausted.

Social Media Post, September 15, 2016

Lyle and I are in the process of sending out our thank-you cards, but we do want to also send out a Facebook thank-you to everyone who has joined us in celebrating our marriage. We appreciate all of the cards, the prayers, the help in getting things together, and the love that has been shown and shared with us both. Thank you, everyone. We love you!

This is not the end of my story. For those of you who have battled cancer, you know that there always seems to be that little voice in the back of your mind that stirs up every time you have a new ache or pain. I am now more aware of my body than I have ever been. I am sure you are as well. I am still projected to be going in for a checkup every three months until I am told otherwise. I also still have to have my port removed. Apparently, it does not get to come out right after you are done with treatments, as I had hoped. It grows on you after a while. I haven't given it much thought lately, but my granddaughter still looks for it daily.

I hope that you have been able to take something away from my story.

*The name of the Lord is a fortified tower; the
righteous run to it and are safe.
—Proverbs 18:10*

I want you to know that knowledge is power. This applies to anything we seek. I thank God for giving me the right words to write *Surviving the Storm*. I thank you for reading this and for supporting the fight against vulvar cancer. It might not be as well-known as some cancers, but any woman who is a part of your life could one day be affected by it.

Written with much love … and keeping the faith.

Me and my number one cheerleader, my love, Lyle.

Peace I leave with you; my peace I give you. I do not give to you as the world gives. Do not let your hearts be troubled and do not be afraid.
—John 14:27

Chapter 20

According to the Centers for Disease Control, 6–7 percent of all gynecological cancers involve the vagina and vulva. That is the percentage for the United States alone. They estimate that each year approximately thirteen hundred women will be diagnosed with vaginal cancer and approximately forty-nine hundred women will be diagnosed with vulvar cancer (Centers for Disease Control and Prevention (CDC) 2016 (revised)). Many times, the problem can be treated before it becomes cancer, because it grows so slowly (The University of Texas MD Anderson Cancer Center 2017). There are many risk factors, but the fact is, since it is so rare, vulvar cancer does not get a lot of attention. Many people don't even know what the vulva is. Many women don't know their own bodies well enough to be concerned. Five thousand women a year is a lot of families being affected. I am sure those people don't feel that it is rare, because it is happening to someone they love, someone they care about. It is time we start taking control of our own health care. We need to be proactive. Women cannot be embarrassed or swayed not to have a manual pelvic exam with their yearly physicals. Suspicious growths or lumps that you may not be aware of could be detected by your physician. So why wouldn't you want to be doing everything possible to ensure you are healthy? Women don't think twice before getting a mammogram these days. Ultimately, we, as the patients, are the ones who need to have a health-care plan we agree upon with our providers. Knowing about vulvar cancer can bring a new awareness to women everywhere. I understand that 6–7 percent seems like a small number. Even if we are shooting for the lowest number, 6 percent of one million is sixty thousand. That is a lot of women being diagnosed and undergoing treatment, with some losing their lives. We are our most ferocious advocates. If something doesn't feel right, we must express the concern. Please don't leave your doctor's office without having your questions answered.

Thank you for joining me on my journey.

Keep the faith and God bless you.

Chapter 21

Written by Dr. Jill Green, family practice physician with MedLogic, LLC

How many people spent this entire book wondering what exactly vulvar cancer was or even what the vulva was? It's okay. It's not a cancer that gets a lot of attention, and it's not a body part that gets a lot of recognition by physicians, but it should. There are no screening guidelines for vulvar cancer, but there is the annual physical exam, which should include not only a breast and gynecological exam but also a discussion of your concerns with your physician. There are so many things we can do in medicine today that are truly feats of scientific progress and magnificence: dialysis for failing kidneys, bypass grafting for clogged coronary arteries, face transplants, test-tube babies, and so on. Nothing is more profound as a medical treatment, though, than prevention. For every medical condition that we can treat, nothing is more effective than preventing it in the first place, and from an economic standpoint, nothing is more cost-effective either. Thus, prevention has profound and far-reaching consequences on our health-care system and on our individual lives.

In order to prevent, we have to be looking for the potential problem. We have to screen for it, like with the mammogram or a pap smear test. Some cancers such as ovarian or pancreatic cancer have no population-based screening. We don't have a reliable or cost-effective way to test the general population for these two cancers. Laura's cancer has no screening program either. Why? Because there simply isn't a blood test, biochemical marker, or imaging study that will identify vulvar cancer easily. As mentioned earlier, Laura's cancer was a "one in a million" for of vulvar cancer. Only a few cases a year in the entire country are identified. Because of its rarity, there is no cost-effective screening process. We don't randomly biopsy the vulva in case there is a cancer. So what should women be doing? Knowledge is power. Educate yourselves. Know your body. Know how to advocate for yourself if you have concerns.

So here we go: what is the vulva?

It surrounds the vagina and includes the labia, clitoris, perineum, Bartholin's glands, and mons pubis. If you don't know what these are, do some research, look them up.

What do you need to know about vulvar cancer? It is incredibly rare: fewer than six thousand new cases per year and about eleven hundred deaths per year.

Most vulvar cancers are SCCs (squamous cell carcinomas). The human papilloma virus (HPV) is strongly linked to SCC-type cancers, as is smoking. Mostly women over sixty are affected, meaning most postmenopausal women, but this is decreasing. We have seen the average age drop significantly over the past decade, most likely due to HPV. Other risk factors include vulvar dystrophy disorders such as lichen sclerosis, immune deficiency disorders, and a history of cervical cancer.

What risk factors are modifiable for this cancer?

Well, we cannot change the fact that women will age, but we can recommend that they stop smoking and get screened for HPV infection by getting pap smears. Likewise, we can recommend that younger women and teens get vaccinated for HPV as early as possible. It is better to be vaccinated before exposure to HPV, which is an extremely common virus with hundreds of different subtypes. The vaccine covers the four to nine most aggressive and dangerous types of this virus, and it is much more effective if you get vaccinated before ever being exposed. This vaccine is recommended for males and females ages nine to twenty-six.

Finally, we can look and we can listen. Physicians need to be able to talk with their patients and perform an effective exam. We, as physicians, cannot hide behind our testing, imaging, and technology and ignore the basics of physical diagnosis. Women should still have an annual gynecological exam. This is recommended by the ACOG (American College of Obstetrics and Gynecology). It's not done enough, and both sides make excuses as to why: no longer sexually active, actively menstruating, embarrassed about hygiene, have had a hysterectomy, or simply feeling like nothing is wrong. Women need an annual exam even if they've had a hysterectomy. There is more anatomy down there than you might think. We need to take care of all of it.

Laura L. Torres

I would like to end with this: when we, as physicians, don't look at your body because we are pressed for time, and you, as our patients, don't talk to us about your concerns because you are uncomfortable, we are doing each other a disservice. Please speak up and ask questions. Please have a full annual physical exam. Please find another doctor if your doctor dismisses your concerns, doesn't answer your questions, or doesn't examine you.

References

Centers for Disease Control and Prevention (CDC). "Vaginal & Vulvar Cancer." *Inside Knowledge: Get the Facts about Gynecologic Cancer.* December 2016 (revised). cdc.gov/cancer/vagvulv/pdf/vagvulv_facts.pdf.

Hume, T., and J. Christensen. "WHO: Imminent Global Cancer 'Disaster' Reflects Aging, Lifestyle Factors." February 4, 2014. cnn.com/2014/02/04/health/who-world-cancer-report/index.html.

Madsen, B. S., H. L. Jensen, A. J. Van Den Brule, et al. "Risk Factors for Invasive Squamous Cell Carcinoma of the Vulva and Vagina-Population Based Case-Control Study in Denmark." *International Journal of Cancer* (2008).

Siegel, R., Z. Zou, and A. Jemal. "Cancer Statistics, 2014." *CA: A Cancer Journal for Clinicians* 64 (January 7, 2014): 9.

The University of Texas MD Anderson Cancer Center. *Vulvar Cancer Facts.* 2017. mdanderson.org/cancer-types/vulvar-cancer/vulvar-cancer-facts.html.

Helpful Resources

Foundation for Women's Cancer
(formerly, Gynecologic Cancer Foundation)
(312) 578-1439
Website: www.foundationforwomenscancer.org

National Cancer Institute
Toll-free number: 1-800-4-CANCER (422-6237)
Website: www.cancer.gov

National Coalition for Cancer Survivorship (NCCS)
1-877-622-7937 (for some publications and Cancer Survivor Toolbox orders)
Website: www.canceradvocacy.org

National Comprehensive Cancer Network
(215) 690-0300
Website: www.nccn.org

American Cancer Society
1-800-227-2345 – helpline
Website: www.cancer.org

CancerCare
1-800-813-HOPE (4673)
Website: www.cancercare.org

The KOSS Family Foundation

Providing financial support for local Racine-area patients battling cancer. Support is for nonmedical expenses such as rent, gas and electric, and other cost-of-living expenses. Bills will be paid directly from the foundation, and gift cards will be supplied for gas and groceries.

Website: www.kossff.org

Froedtert & the Medical College of Wisconsin Cancer Center
Website: www.froedtert.com/cancer

The YMCA Livestrong Program

A twelve-week program provided free to cancer survivors (either finished with or going through active treatments). The program meets twice weekly and includes a three-month YMCA membership for participants and their families while they are enrolled in the program. It is necessary to apply for this at the YMCA and obtain a physician's release for participation. The program focuses on strength training, flexibility, and the overall ability to function, as well as providing a supportive environment for participants' emotional health. To obtain information about this program in the Racine area, go to www.ymcaracine.org. For information about the program in other locations, contact your local YMCA.

Graduation party for 2016 Livestrong program participants at the YMCA.